How to Draw Superheros (This Book Includes Superhero Girls, Information on How to Draw Superheros Step by Step, and How to Draw a Superhero in 3D)

This Superhero Drawing Book has 40 Superheros to Learn to Draw and is Suitable for Kids Aged 9-12

James Manning

HOW TO DRAW SUPERHEROES

Introduction

Drawing stimulates parts of the brain that are responsible for creative thinking and imagination. From a young age, we are all creatively encouraged to draw, often to improve our fine motor skills and co-ordination.

From toddler 'scribbles' to 'matchstick men' you may find that as you get older you will want to tackle more complex drawings (perhaps it's an image you have seen in a book) but as you begin to put pencil to paper you may have no idea where to start, causing you frustration and annoyance.

With the help of our 'How to Draw' book series, this frustration will disappear as we guide you step by step, line by line, to create your very own masterpieces!

Each illustration in this book is deconstructed and simplified into lines and shapes that will not overwhelm you. As we guide you to form each simple line and shape together on the paper, the image gradually becomes more detailed and textured.

There will be such a sense of accomplishment and achievement once your drawing is complete, which in turn will boost your self-esteem and confidence.

Drawing Characters Step-by-Step

For the rest of the book I will show you how to draw 40 different characters step by step. Each step will build on the previous step until eventually you have 40 complete characters.

If at first, you find my step-by-step approach too complicated or difficult please leave it to one side and come back to it later. Instead, use the grids with numbers and letters on it first. By following the coordinates and matching them up with the coordinates on a blank grid you can redraw the characters that way instead.

What to do if you get frustrated whilst drawing

You may find that whilst working through my 'How to Draw' series, you may become frustrated as you find learning the new skill harder than you may have first anticipated. What you have drawn on the paper may be different to how you envisioned it to look, or you may be constantly comparing your skill to friends and siblings efforts. Learning a brand new skill can be difficult and time consuming, and you will need to remind yourself that everyone learns and works at different paces and that it is perfectly fine for you to take your time in refining your new skill.

If you find that your concentration is lost and you become agitated and frustrated with your work, it is very important to try and keep the activity fun and engaging, so encouraging regular breaks is imperative. It may even be better to encourage yourself to do a completely different activity for a while and come back to drawing tomorrow.

Validating your feelings is also crucial. It is okay for you to feel annoyed and frustrated, but always encourage yourself to keep trying. Perhaps tell yourself to take a step back in the book and repeat a part that they you have already mastered, then gradually move onto the step that you are finding trickier.

Everyone, including adults and the most successful artists can make mistakes, and sometimes these mistakes could even be successes! The extra line or shape you may have drawn accidently, could become part of the drawing as a whole and copying the lines exactly as they are in the book isn't a necessity.

However, drawing in pencil, rather than permanent ink, allows any 'mistakes' to be erased and learnt from. Being able to remove what you feel is a mistake will stop you from feeling overwhelmed and that you must start over from the beginning; instead you can carry on from the point you were able to erase out.

Try to always reinforce to yourself that the best way to learn when drawing is to learn from mistakes and continue on.

J.P Manning

HOW TO DRAW SUPERHEROES

Here are all of the characters in this book. I guess it must seem like there is a lot of them when they are looked at all at once!

Luckily, I am not going to ask you to draw them all straight away. The best way to learn to draw is one step at a time. Each character in this book may require between 50 and 100 strokes of your pencil, but all you will need to think about is drawing one stroke at a time.

As you use your pencil, stroke by stroke, working your way through this book, you will eventually be able to draw all of the characters!

1. Ellipses on your initial grid can be
used to help you draw characters
with a 3D effect.

A B C D E F G H

2. Drawing a basic grid outline will help you to give your picture good proportions.

A B C D E F G H
1
2
3
4
5
6
7
8
9
10
11
12

3. Starting your drawing with the eyes will help your initial sketch to take shape.

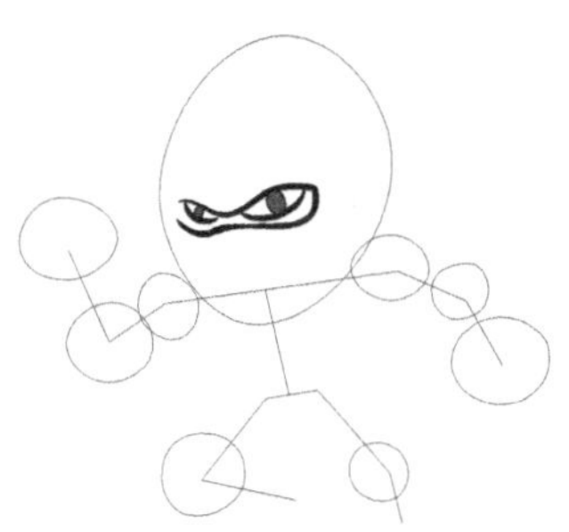

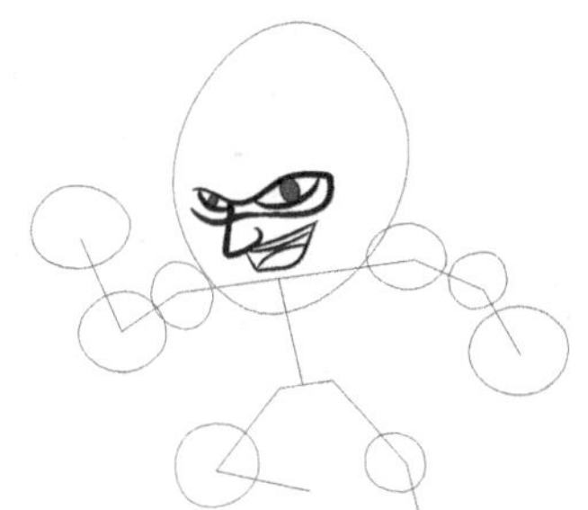

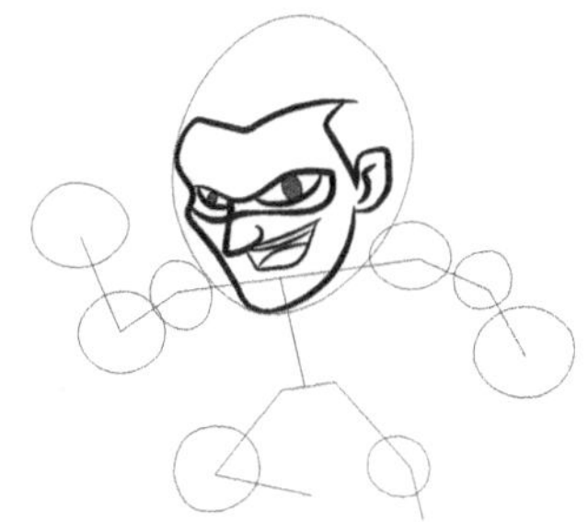

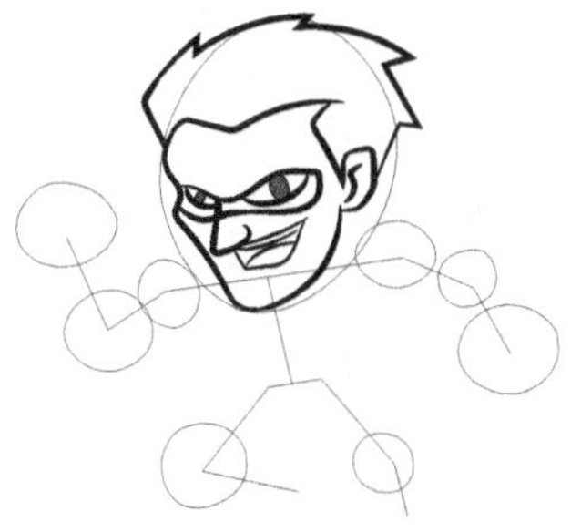

A B C D E F G H
1
2
3
4
5
6
7
8
9
10
11
12

4. Separate your grid into sections to help you decide how you want to proportion your drawing.

A B C D E F G H
1
2
3
4
5
6
7
8
9
10
11
12

5. You can create 3D type effects by enlarging some body parts and making other body parts smaller.

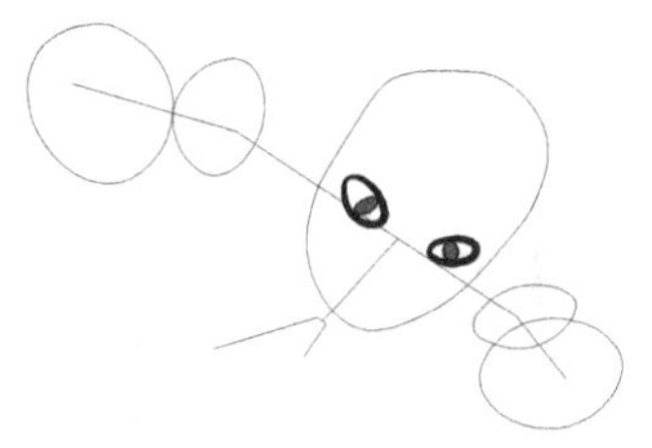

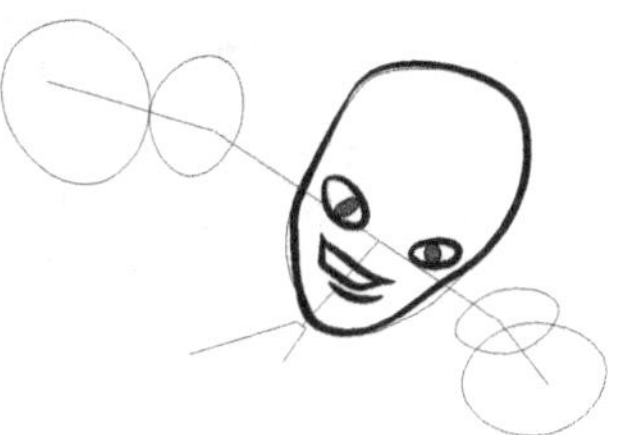

A B C D E F G H

6. Drawing eyes closer together can
make the character you are drawing
look angrier.

A B C D E F G H
1
2
3
4
5
6
7
8
9
10
11
12

7. Separate your grid into
sections to help you decide
how you want to proportion
your drawing. This can help
you to alter the height of
your character.

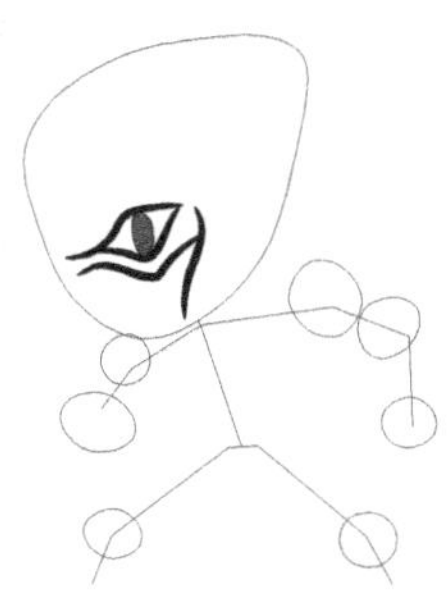

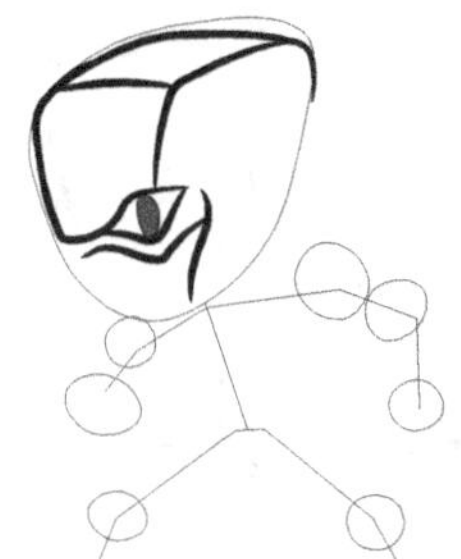

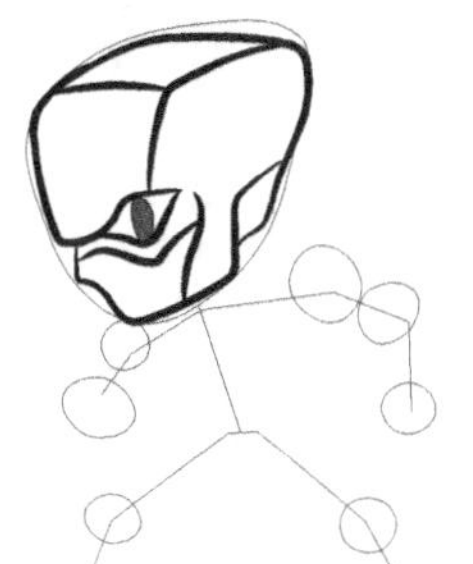

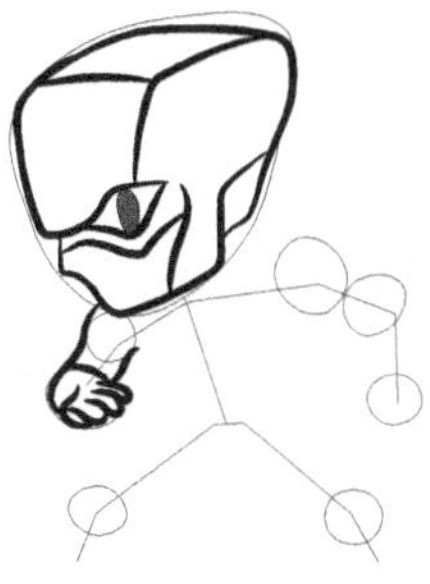

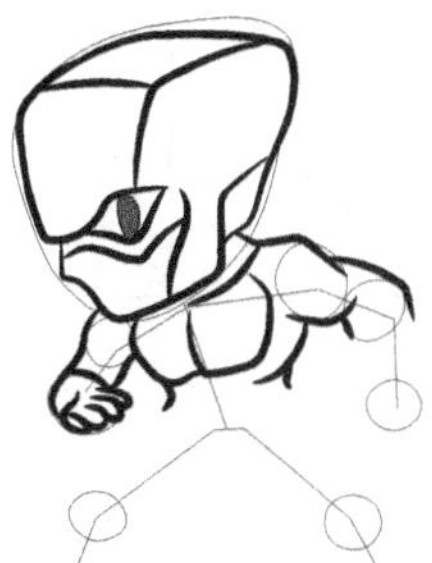

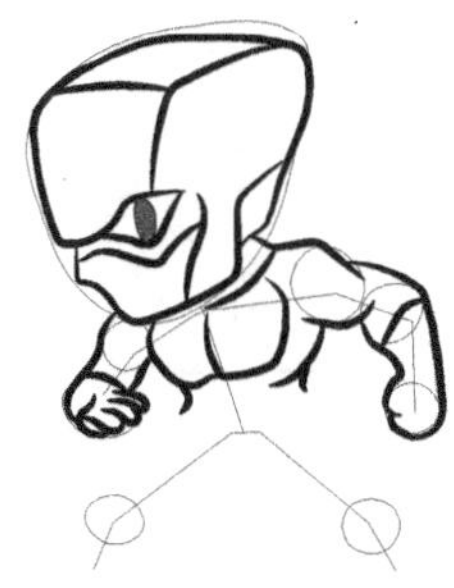

A B C D E F G H
1
2
3
4
5
6
7
8
9
10
11
12

8. Starting your drawing with the eyes will help your initial sketch to take shape. Follow that by constructing the head.

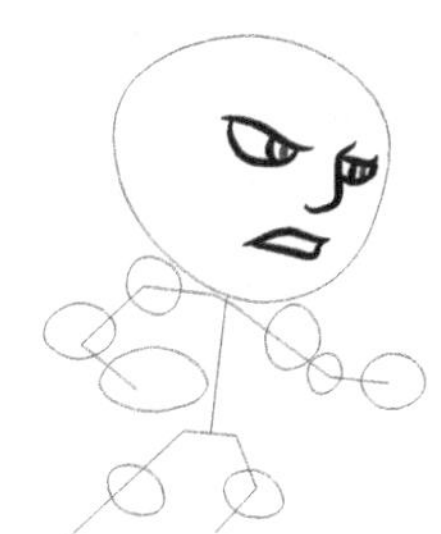

A B C D E F G H
1
2
3
4
5
6
7
8
9
10
11
12

9. After you have drawn
your character's head it is
easier to add small details.

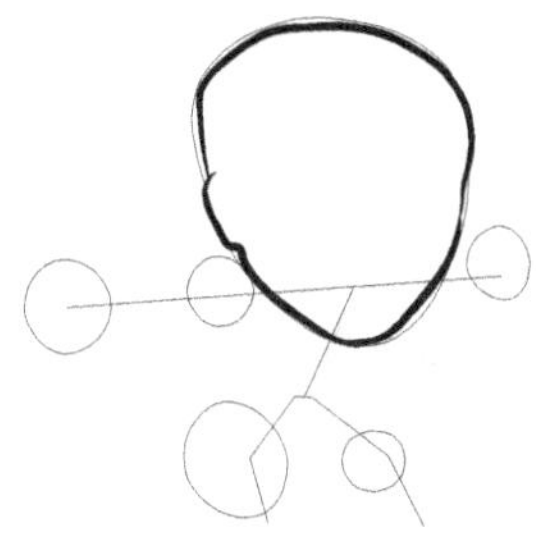 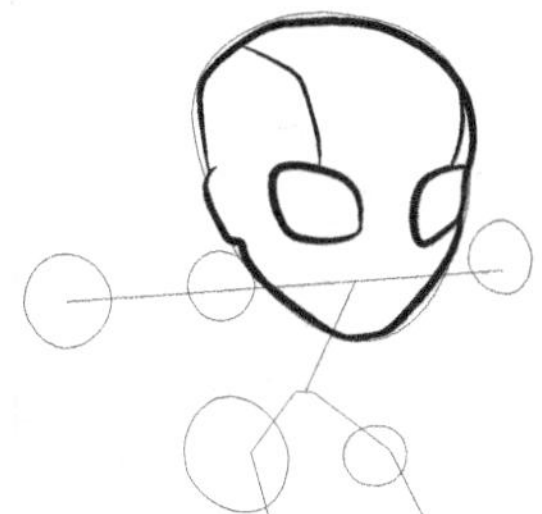 

A B C D E F G H
1
2
3
4
5
6
7
8
9
10
11
12

10. You can change your character's features by making small adjustments.

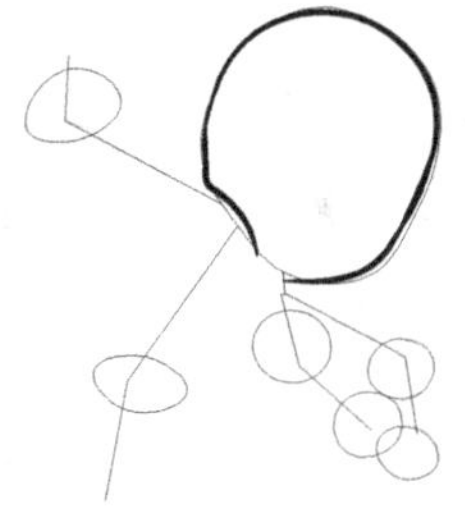

A B C D E F G H
1
2
3
4
5
6
7
8
9
10
11
12

11. Try altering your grid to make
your character shorter or taller.

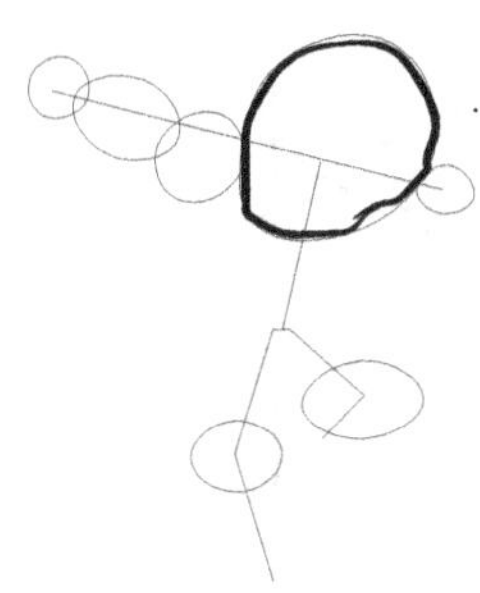 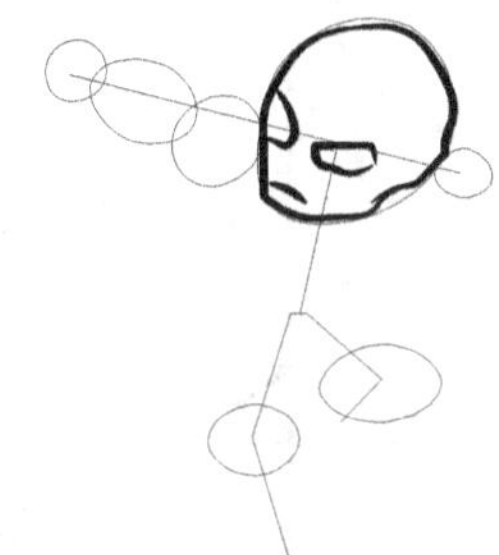 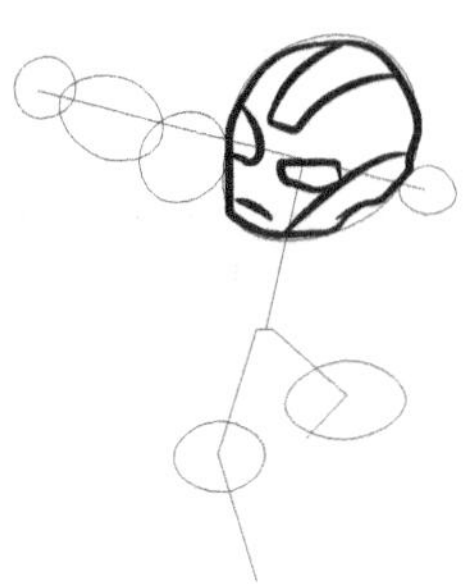

 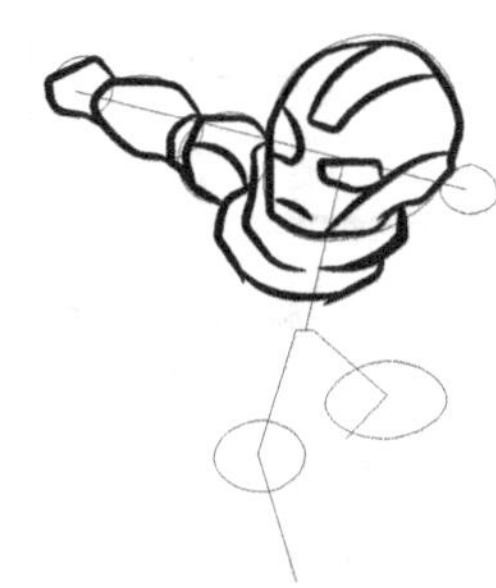 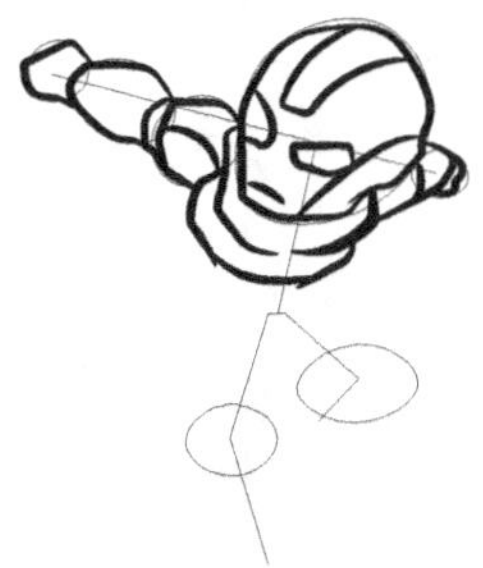

A B C D E F G H
1
2
3
4
5
6
7
8
9
10
11
12

12. Increasing the size of your character's head can make it look more childlike.

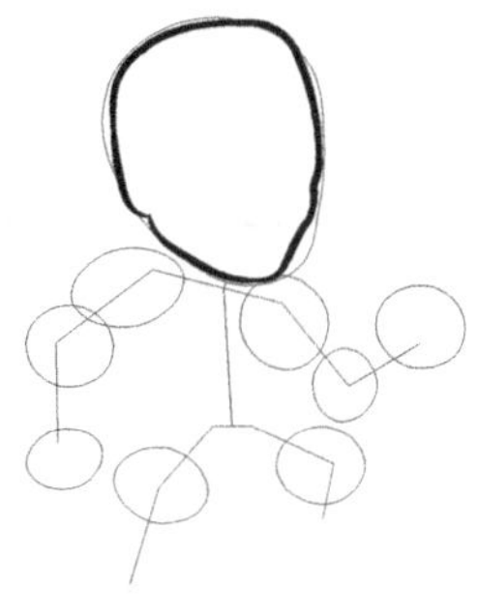

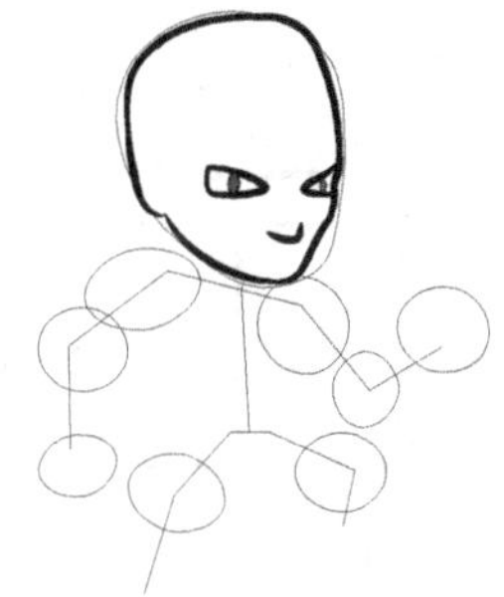

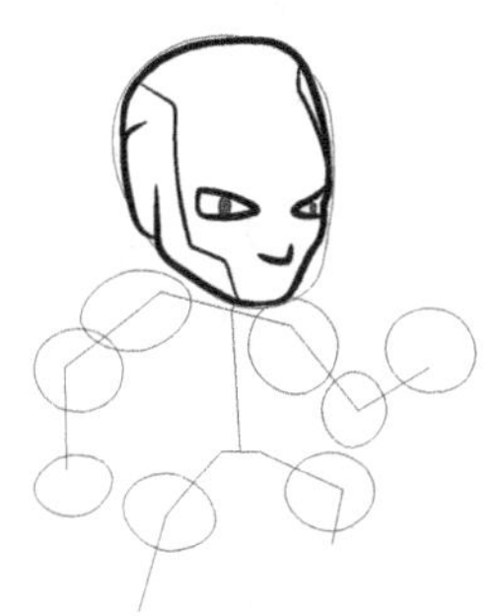

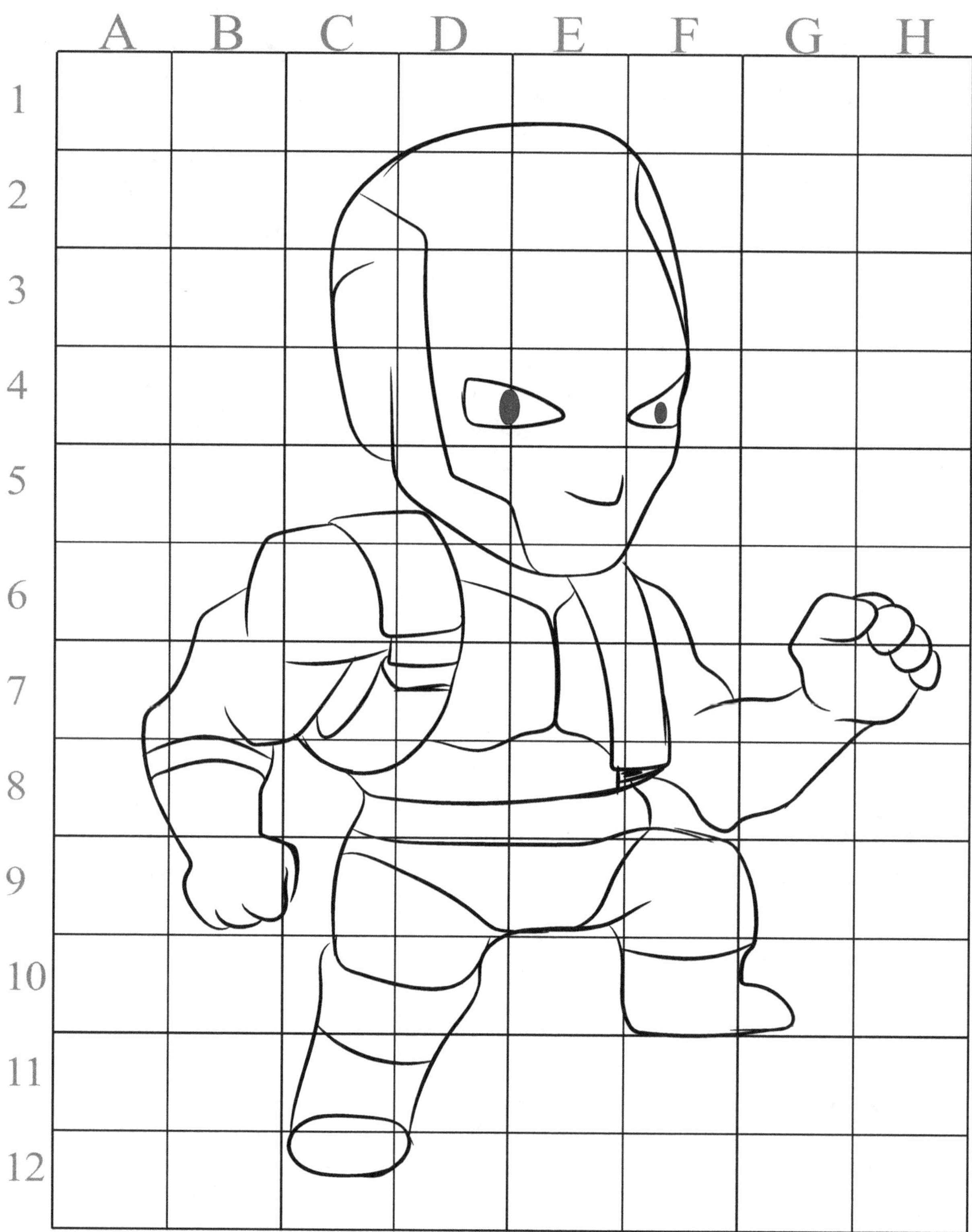

A B C D E F G H
1 2 3 4 5 6 7 8 9 10 11 12

13. Here is another example of a 3D effect.

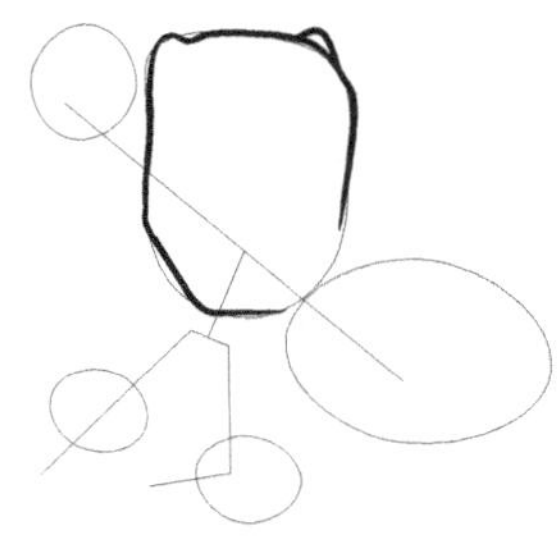
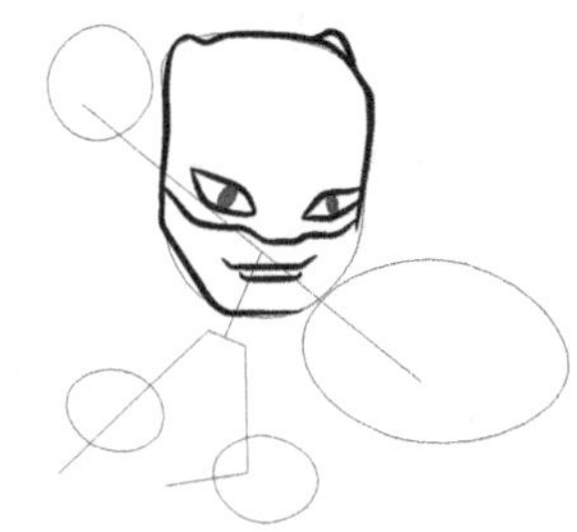

A B C D E F G H
1
2
3
4
5
6
7
8
9
10
11
12

14. Add extra details to
your drawings to make
more unique characters.

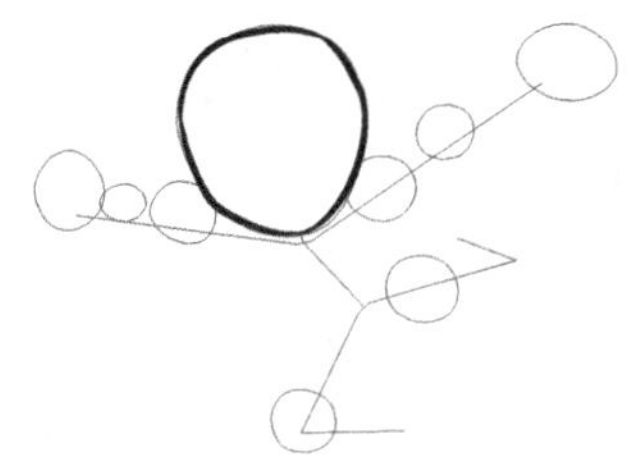

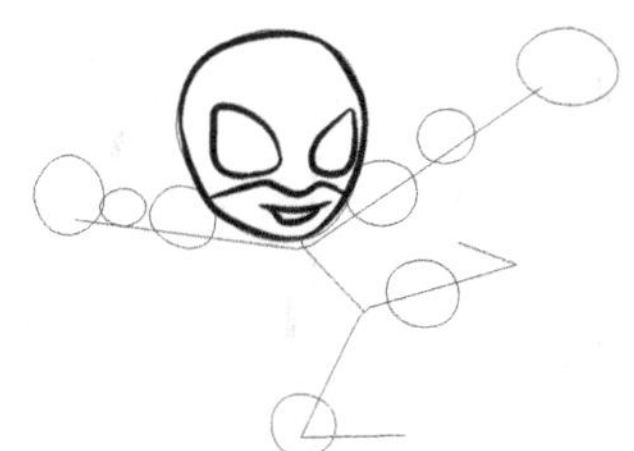

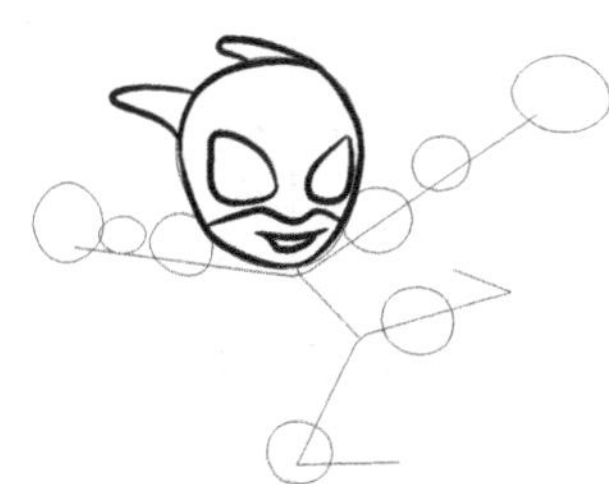

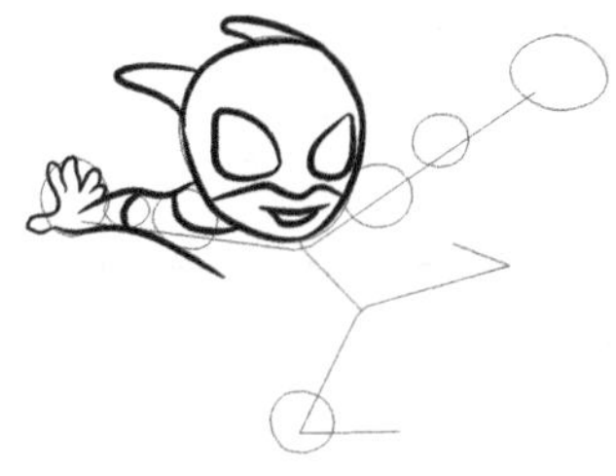

A B C D E F G H
1
2
3
4
5
6
7
8
9
10
11
12

15. Drawing is a process of
construction. Add one
small part at a time.

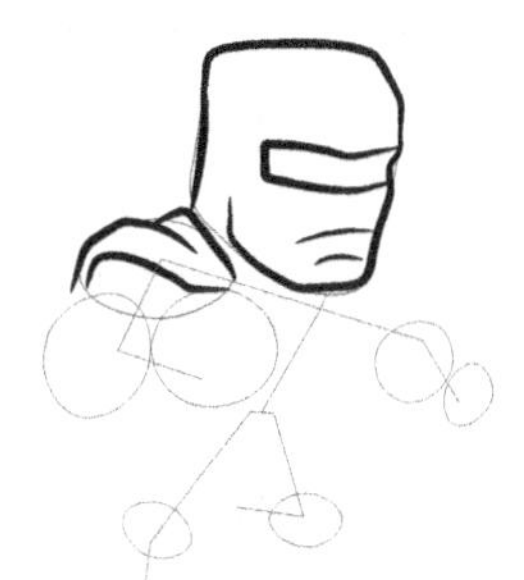

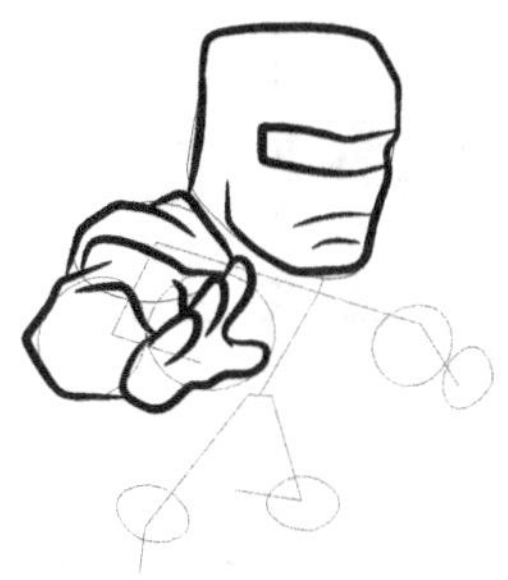

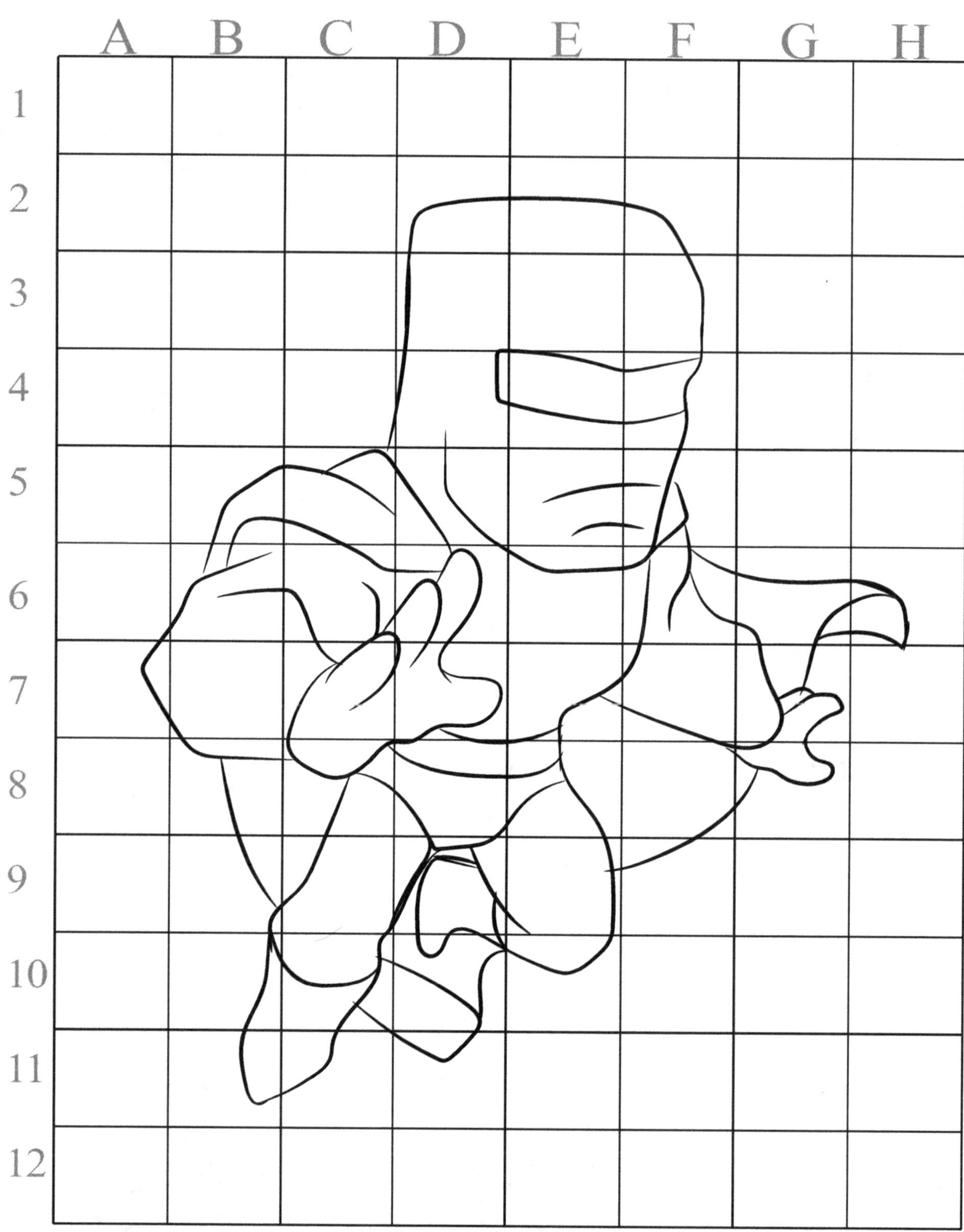

16. It can be very difficult to get things right the first time, but remember the more you draw the better you will get at it.

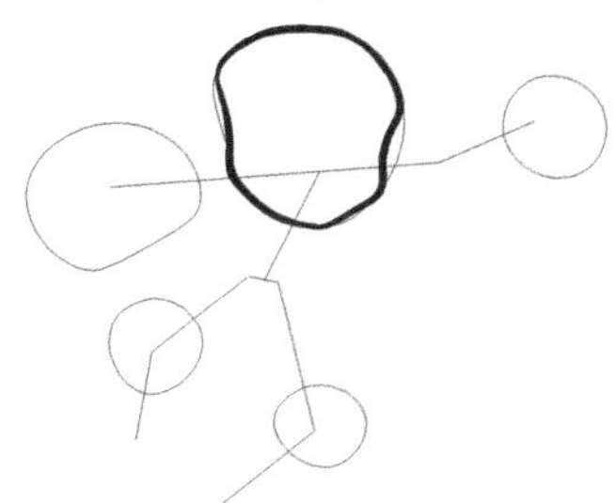

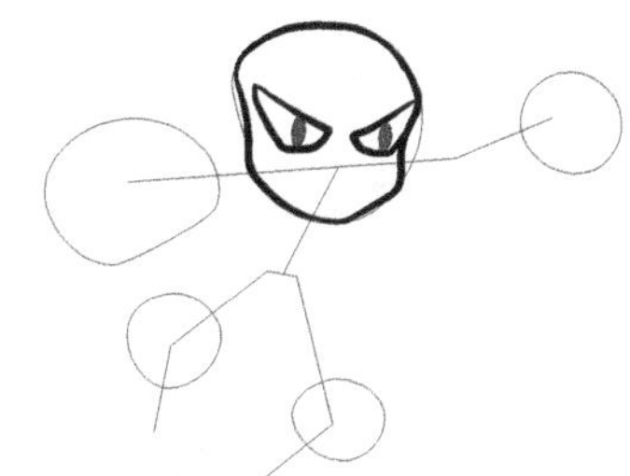

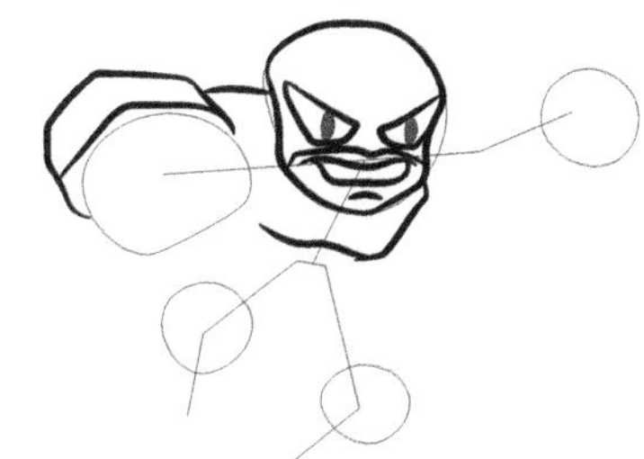

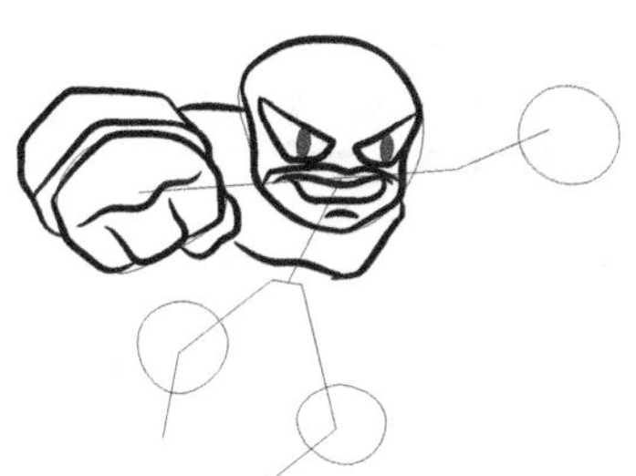

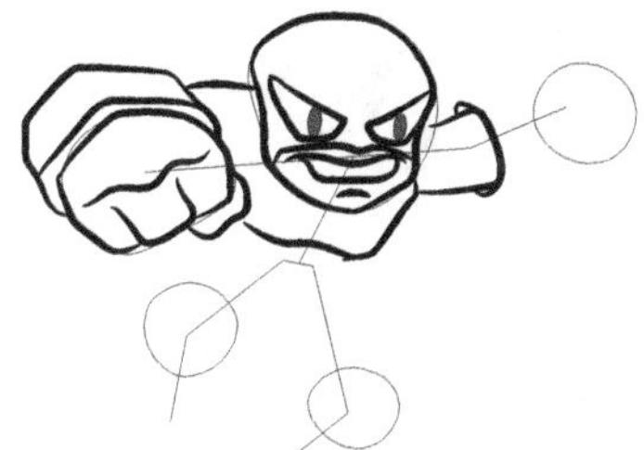

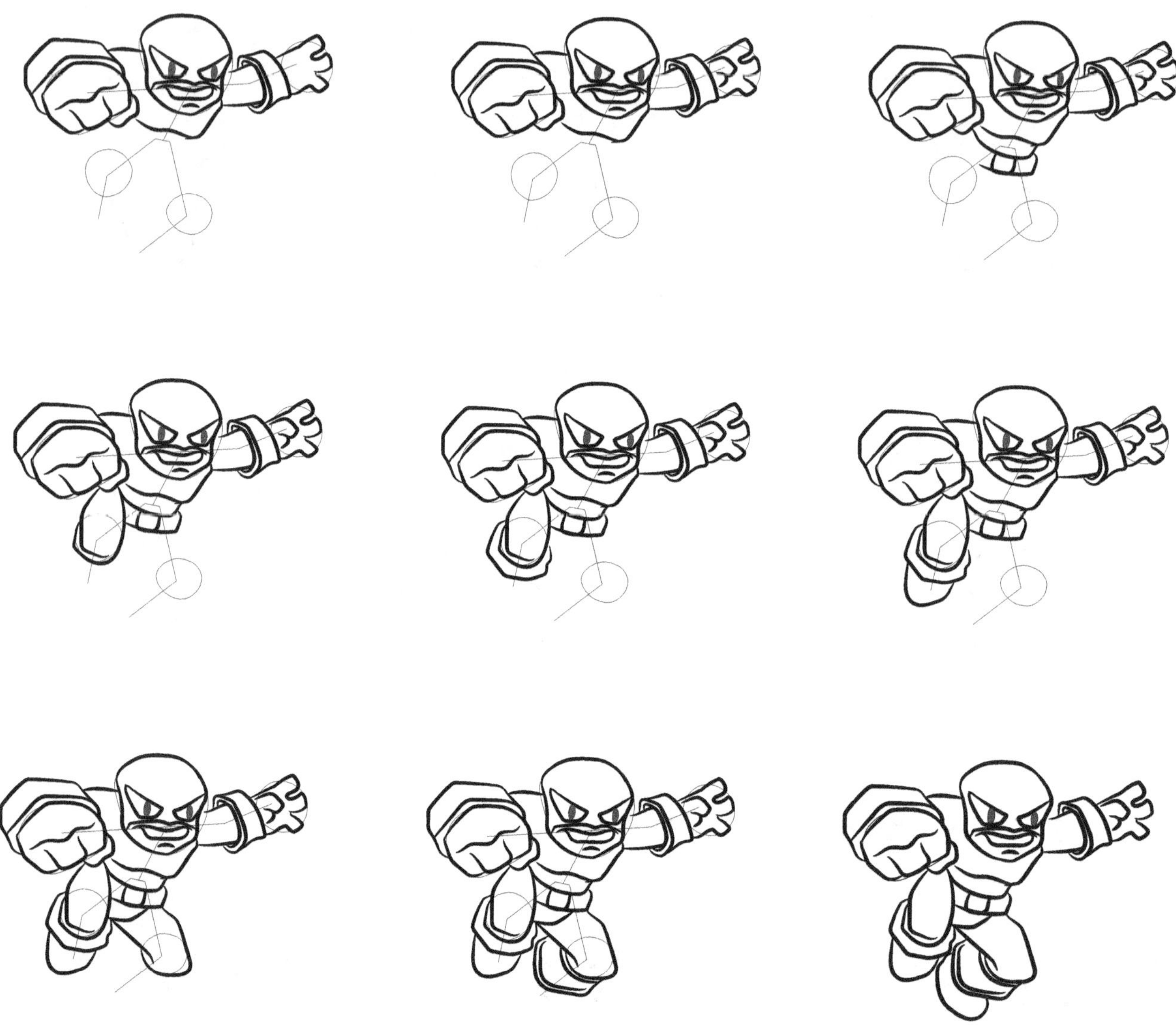

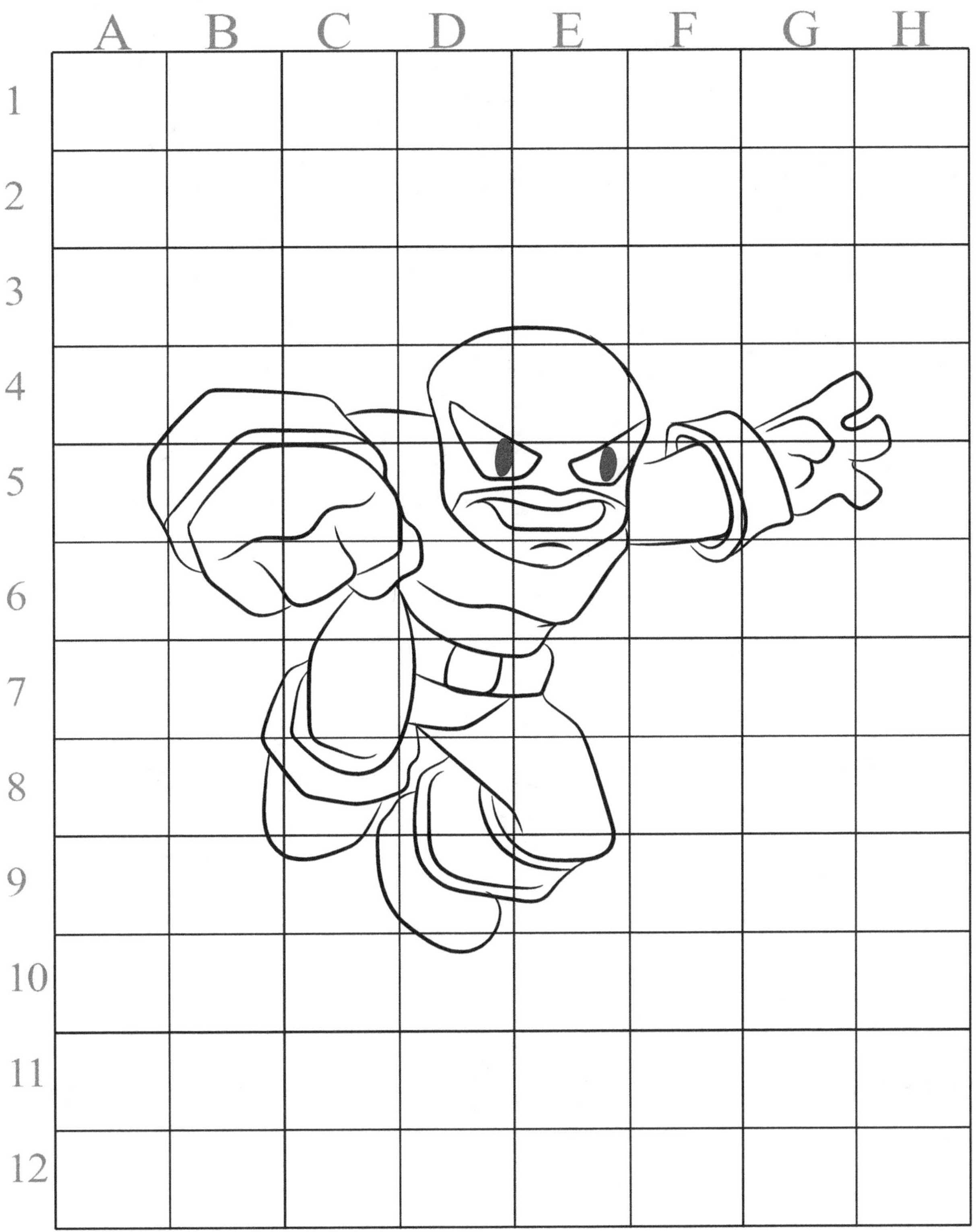

A B C D E F G H
1
2
3
4
5
6
7
8
9
10
11
12

17. Try swapping the
head of your character
for another head in this
book. This can lead to
very interesting creations.

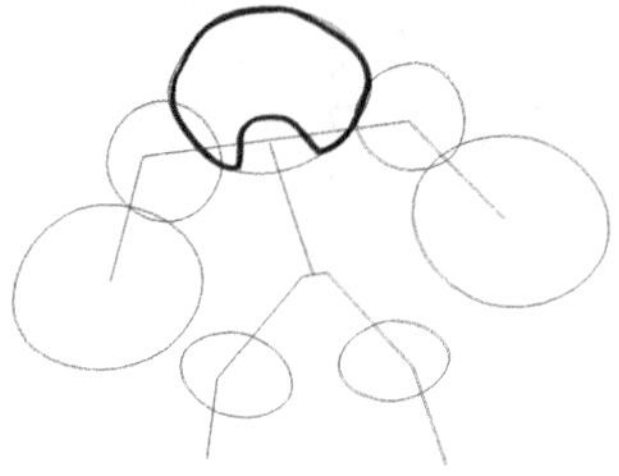

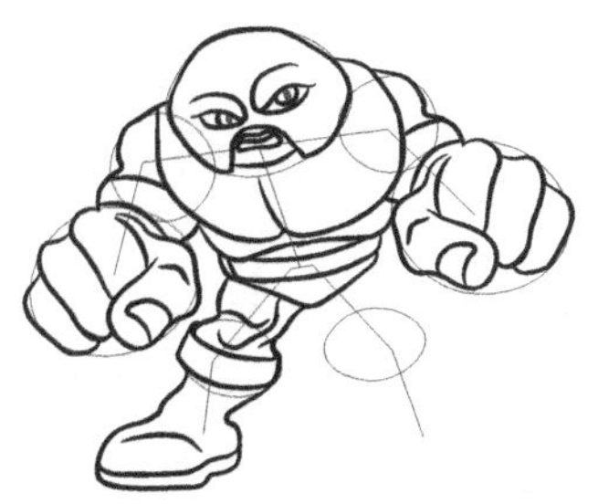

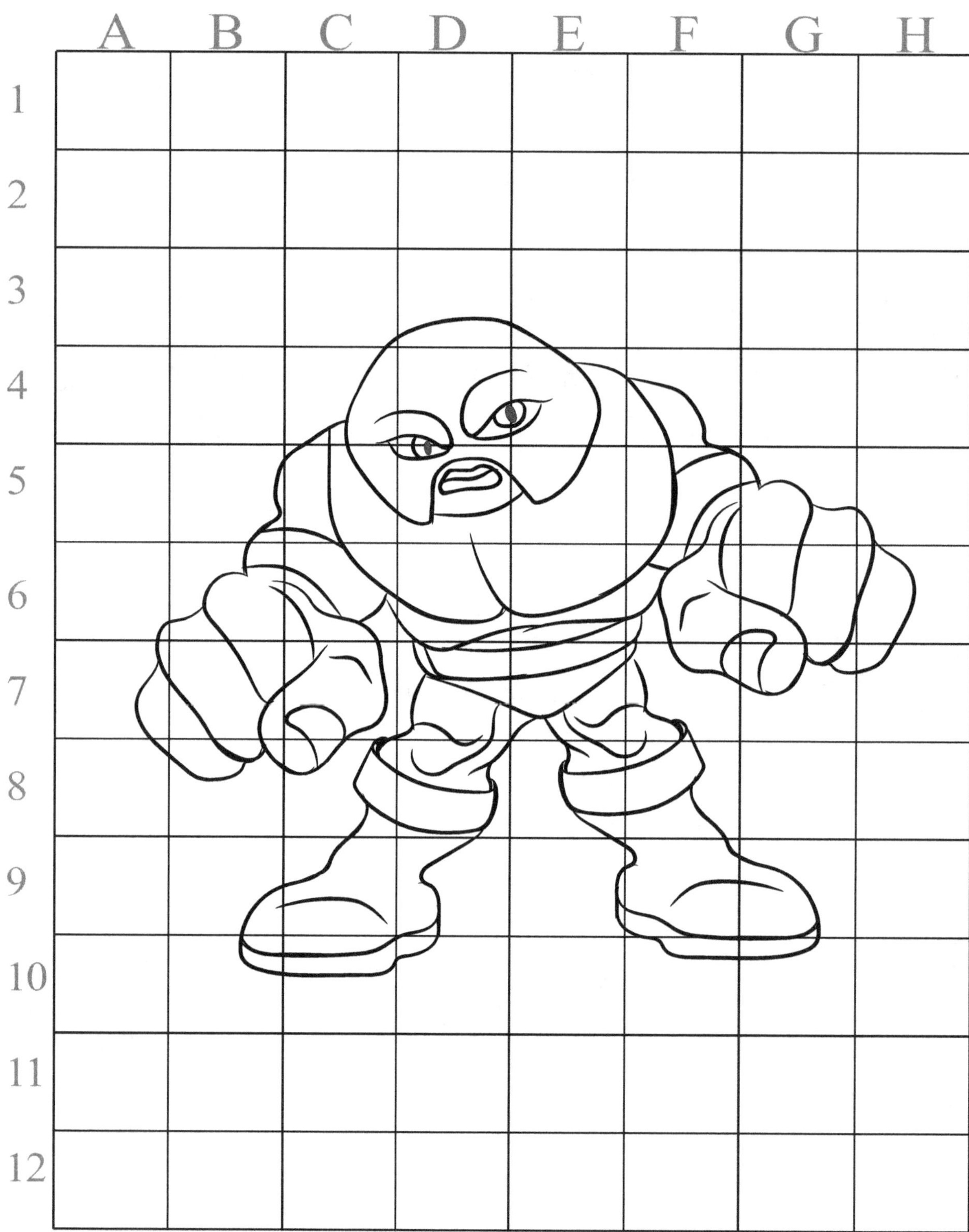

18. To become an expert at something you may need to spend thousands of hours doing it. Expert artists often will often have spent more than 10,000 hours practising.

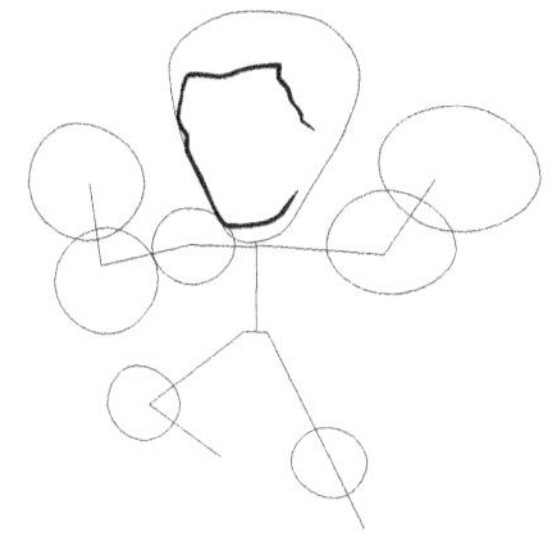  

 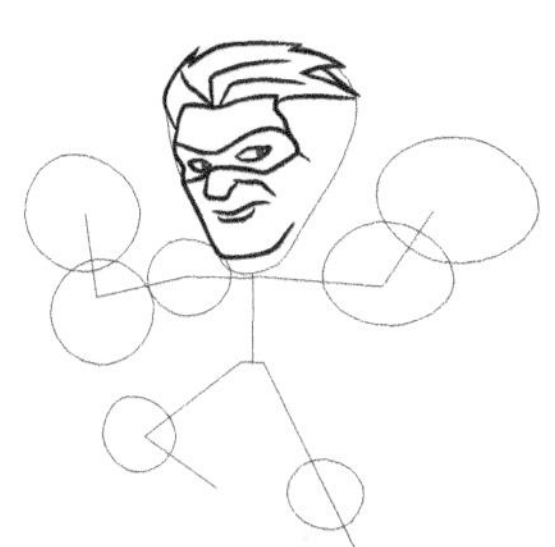 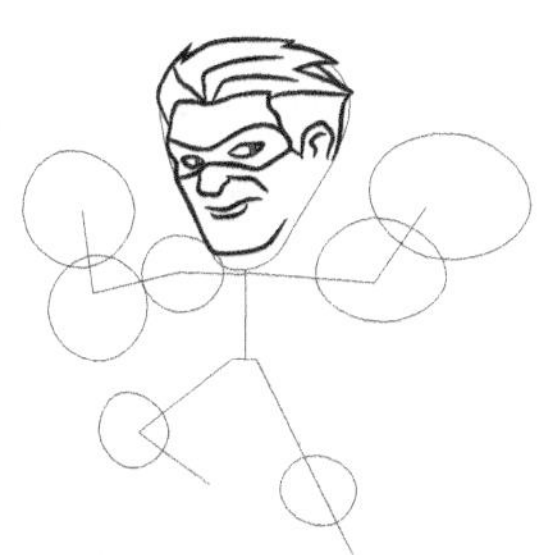

A B C D E F G H
1
2
3
4
5
6
7
8
9
10
11
12

19. We all make mistakes, even the
most successful people in life do.
What sets successful people apart is
how they respond to their mistakes.

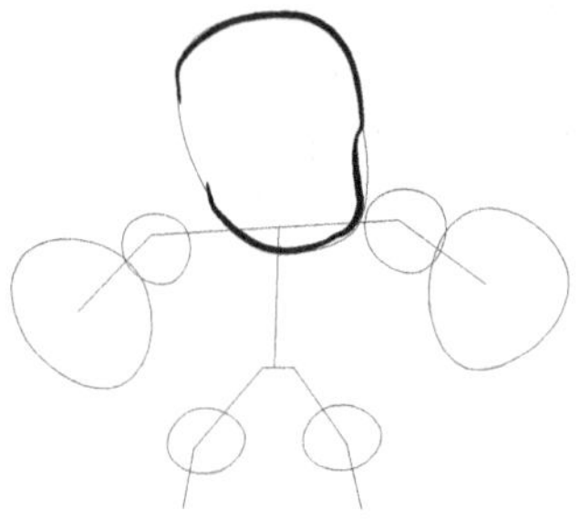

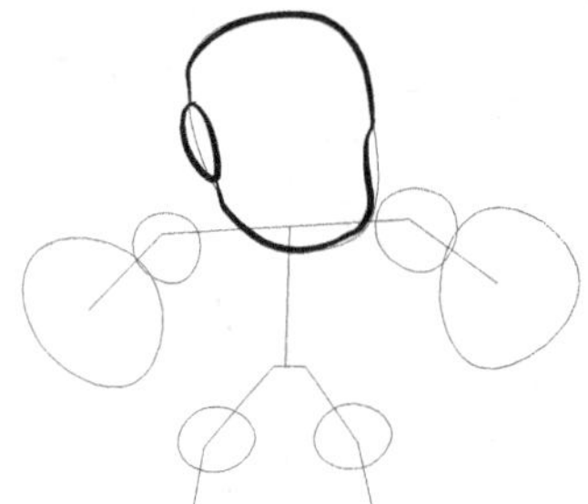

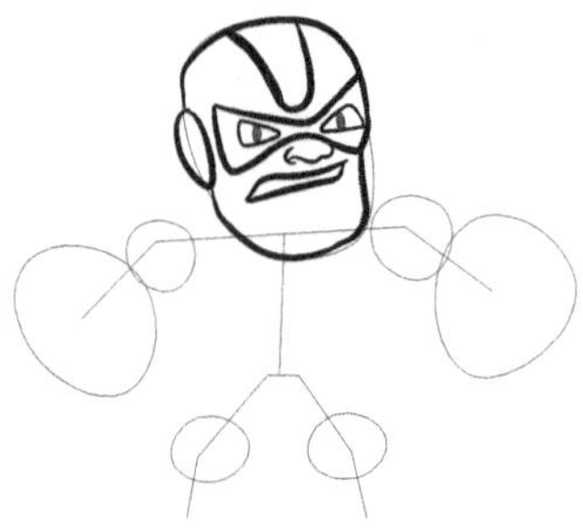

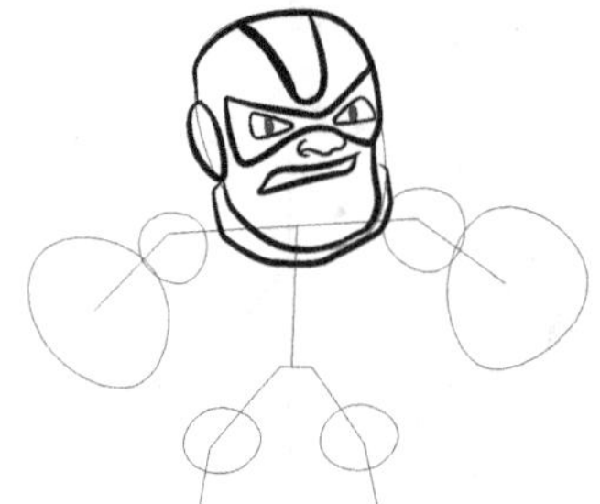

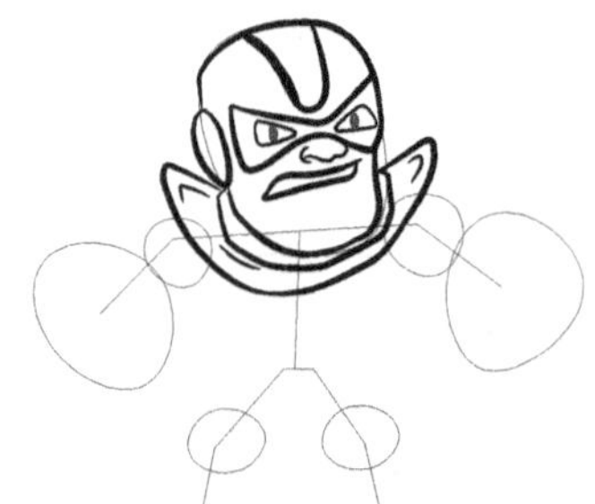

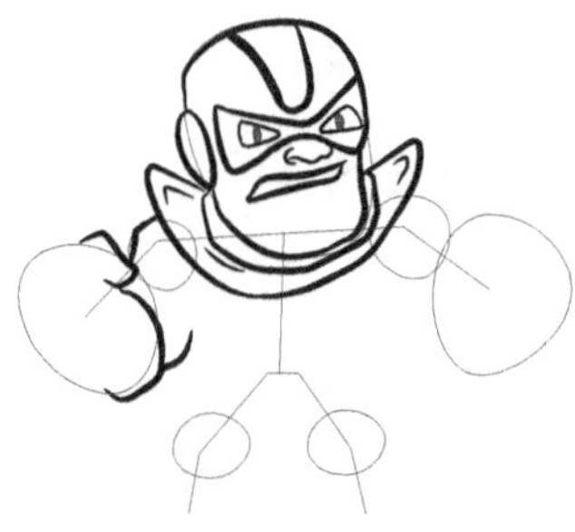

A B C D E F G H
1
2
3
4
5
6
7
8
9
10
11
12

20. You can make a character look as though it is being looked down upon from above by increasing the size of the upper body in comparison to the lower body.

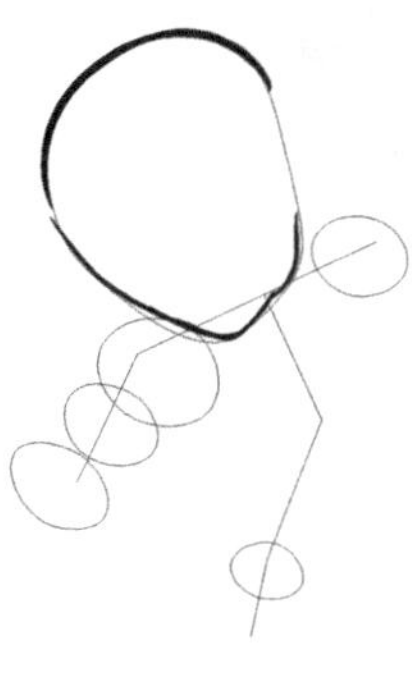

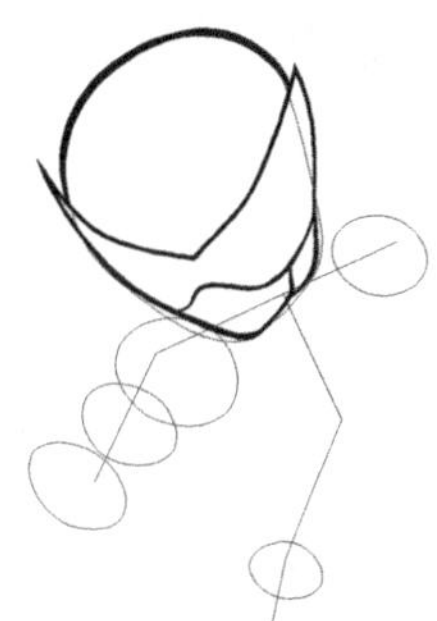

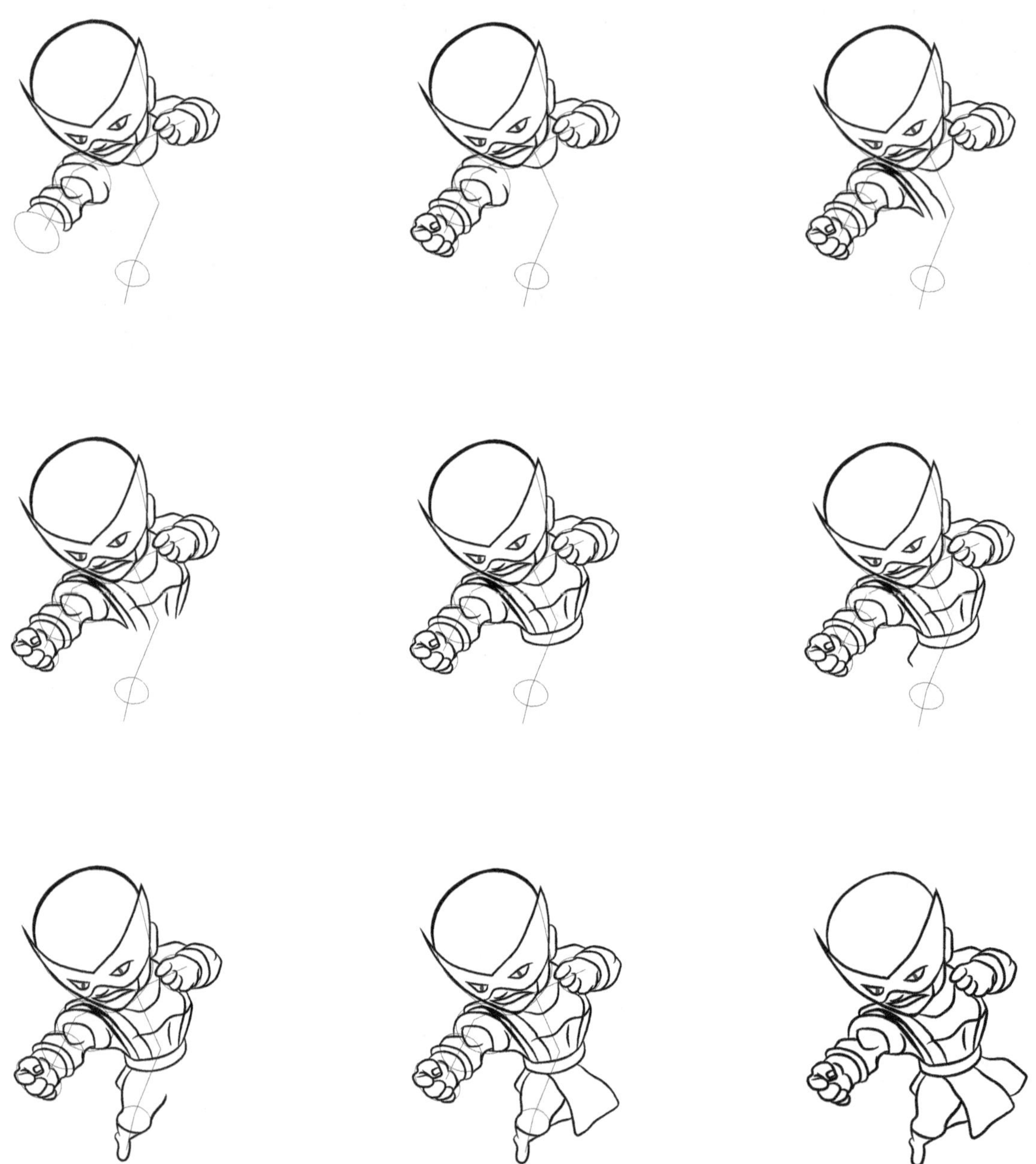

A B C D E F G H
1 2 3 4 5 6 7 8 9 10 11 12

21. For larger projects focus on one
step at a time. People have walked
thousands of miles by taking one step
at a time.

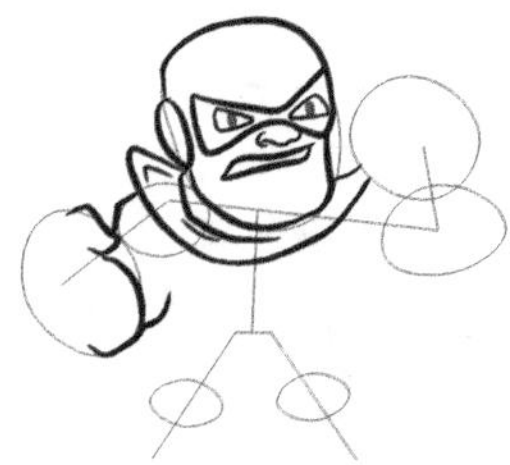

22. Drawing eyes further apart can make
your character look more relaxed.

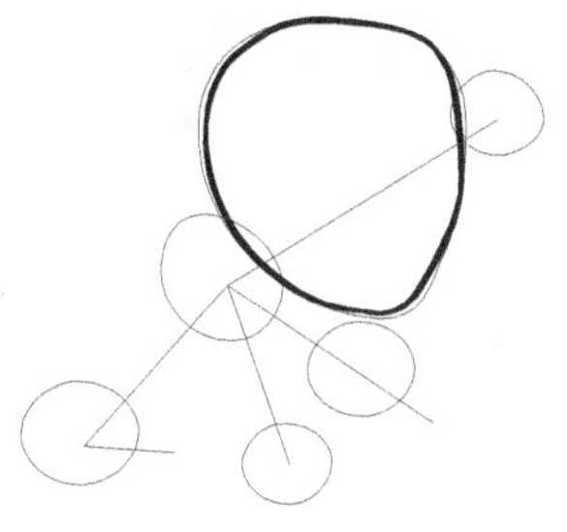 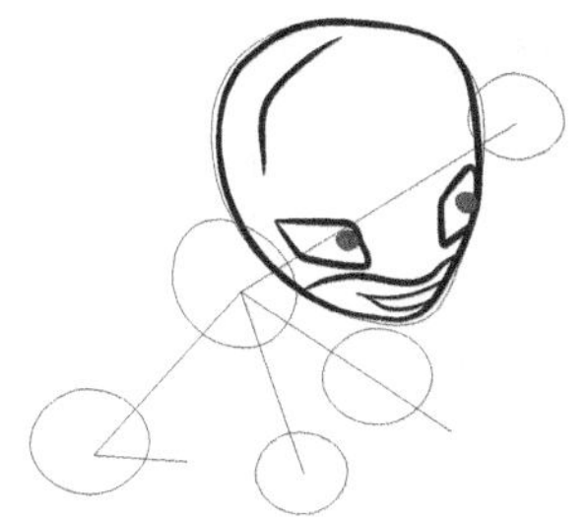 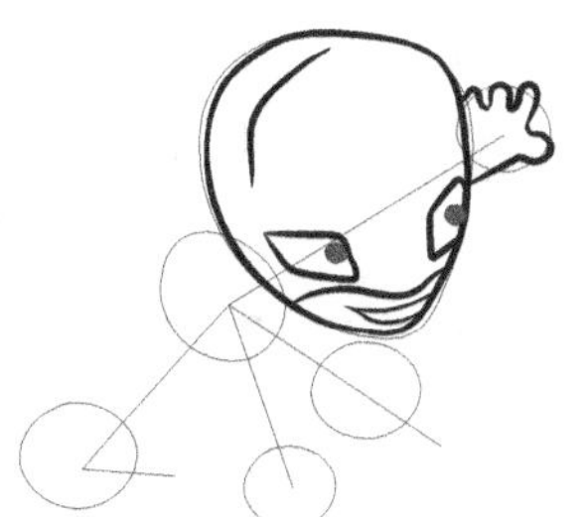

 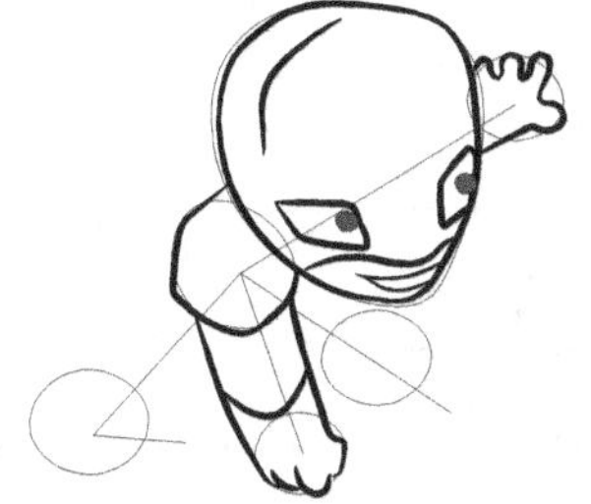 

A B C D E F G H
1
2
3
4
5
6
7
8
9
10
11
12

23. Here is another
example of a 3D effect.

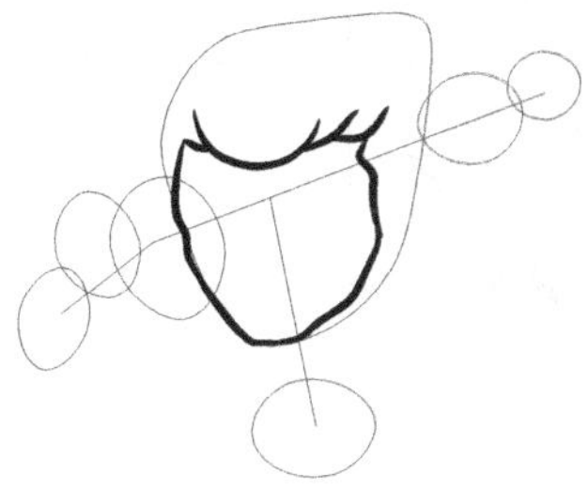

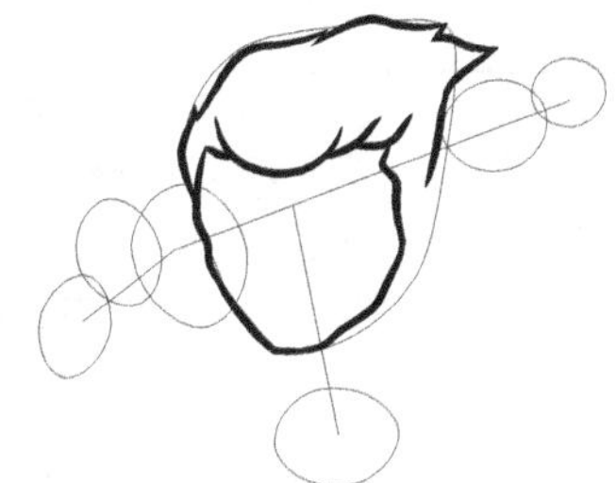

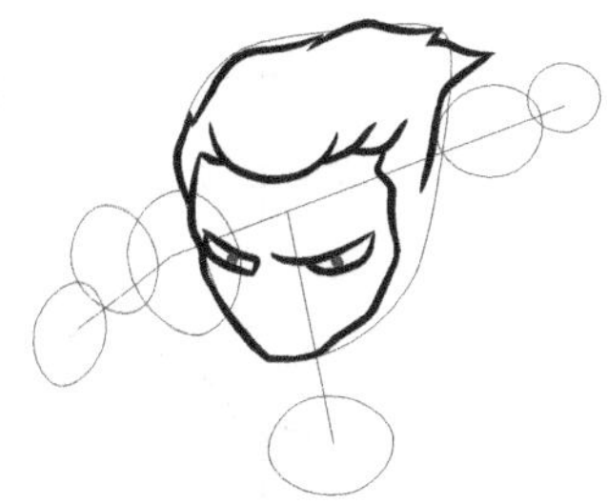

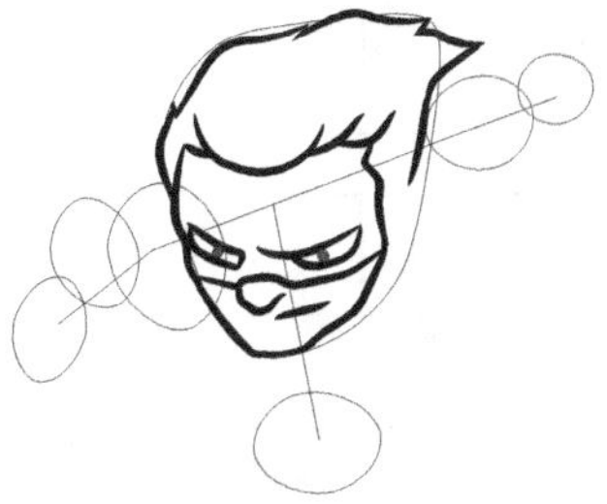

A B C D E F G H

24. Giving your character large eyes and a small nose and mouth will make your character look more innocent and childlike.

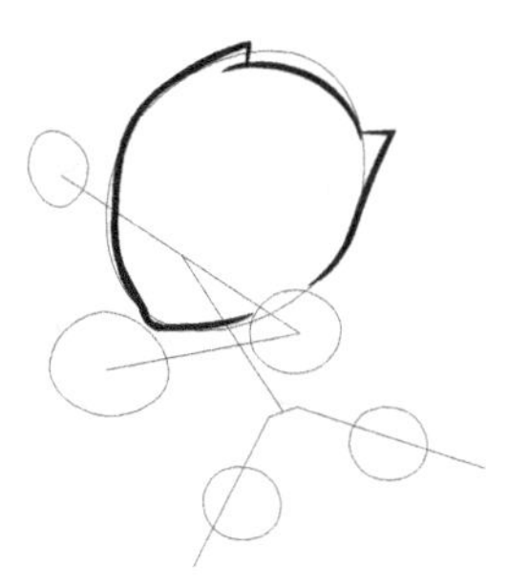 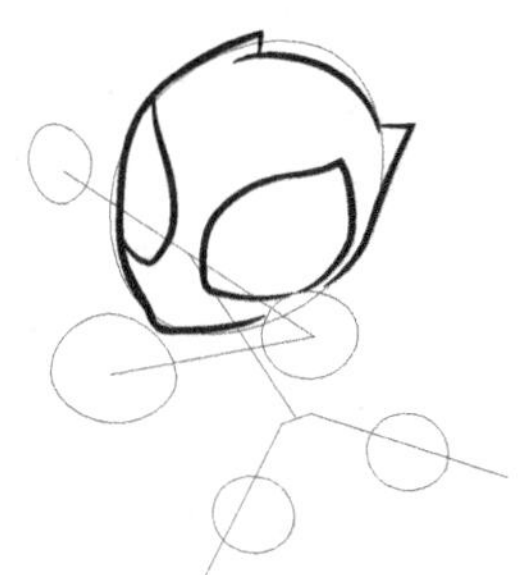 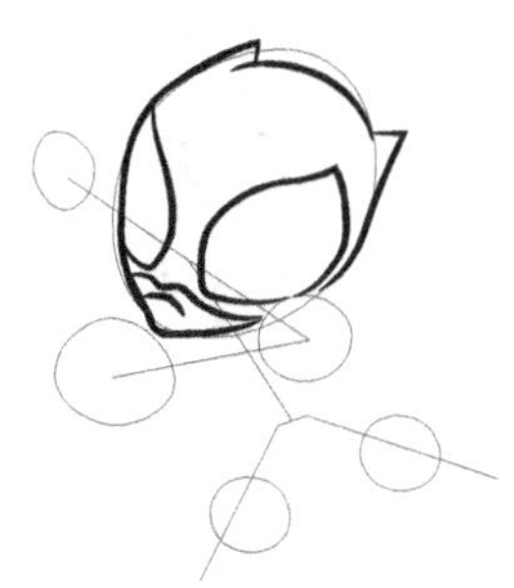

A B C D E F G H
1 2 3 4 5 6 7 8 9 10 11 12

25. It is very rare to see characters that are exactly alike. It is usually small details that separate them.

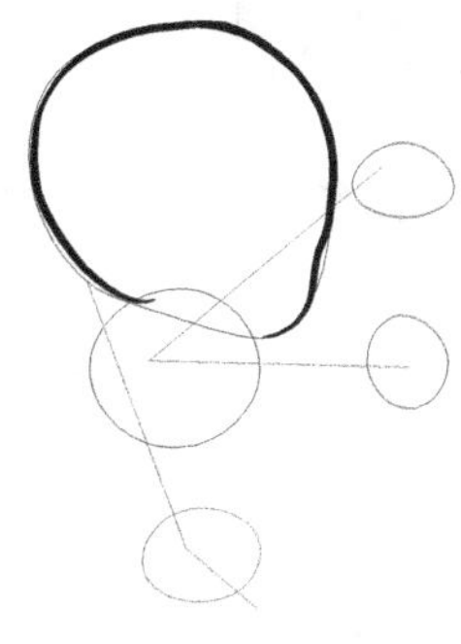

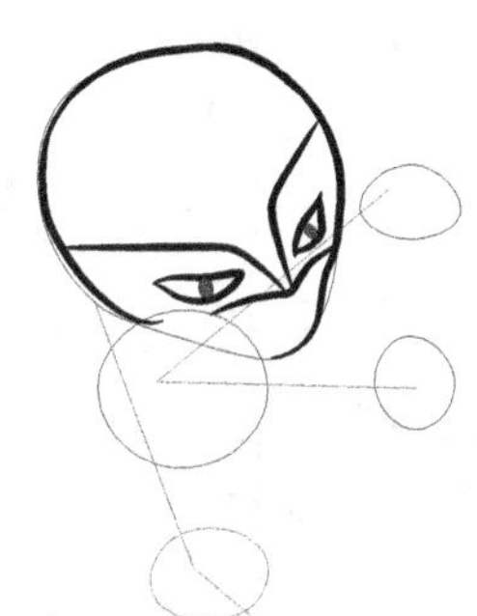

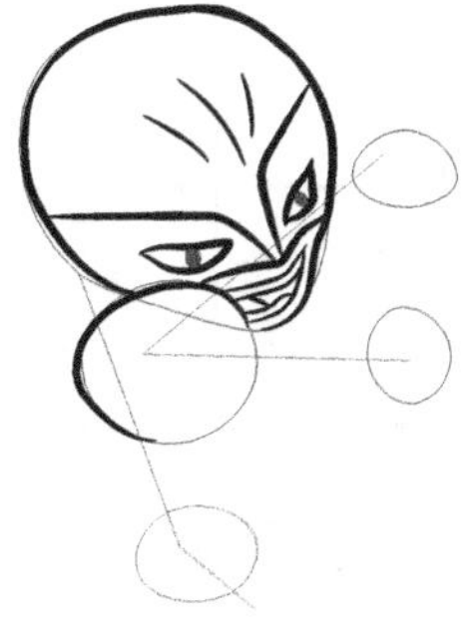

A B C D E F G H
1
2
3
4
5
6
7
8
9
10
11
12

26. To draw a mirror
image of your character
draw everything the
opposite way.

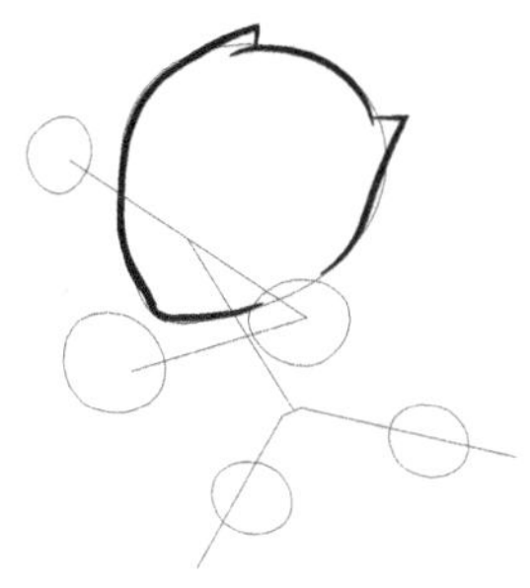

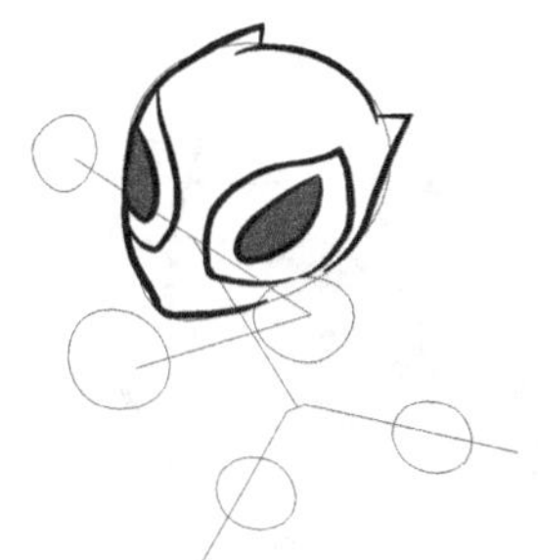

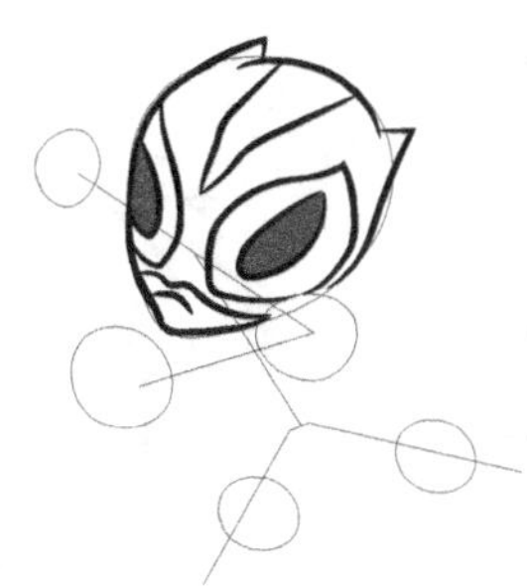

A B C D E F G H
1
2
3
4
5
6
7
8
9
10
11
12

27. Once you become more
experienced at drawing, you can draw
your own grids.

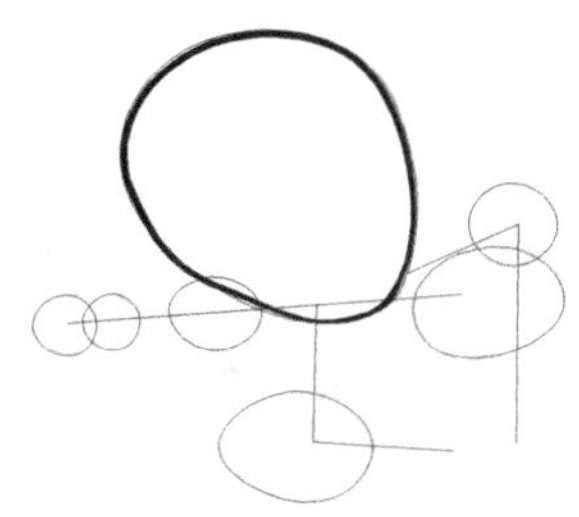
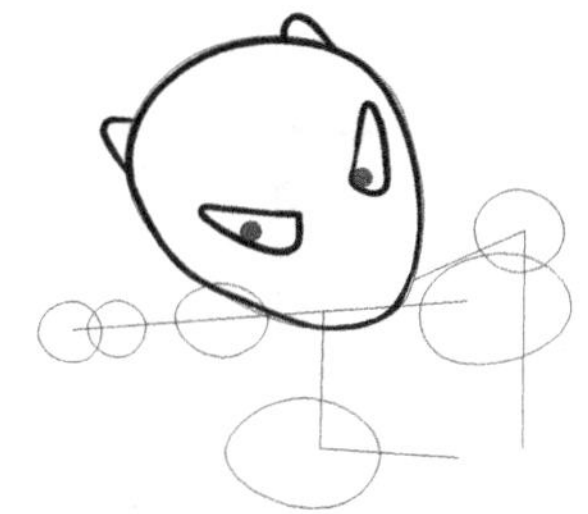
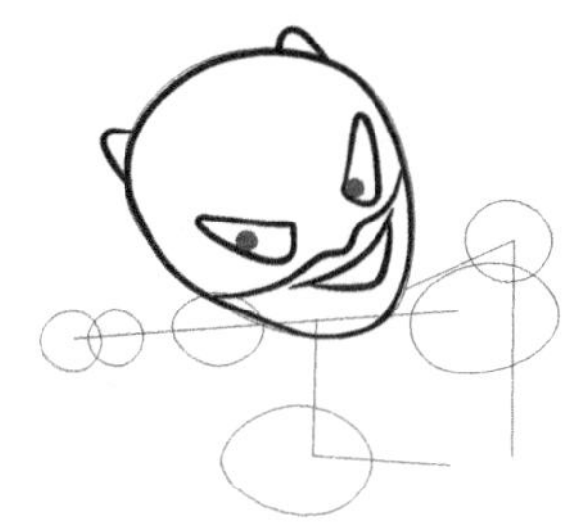

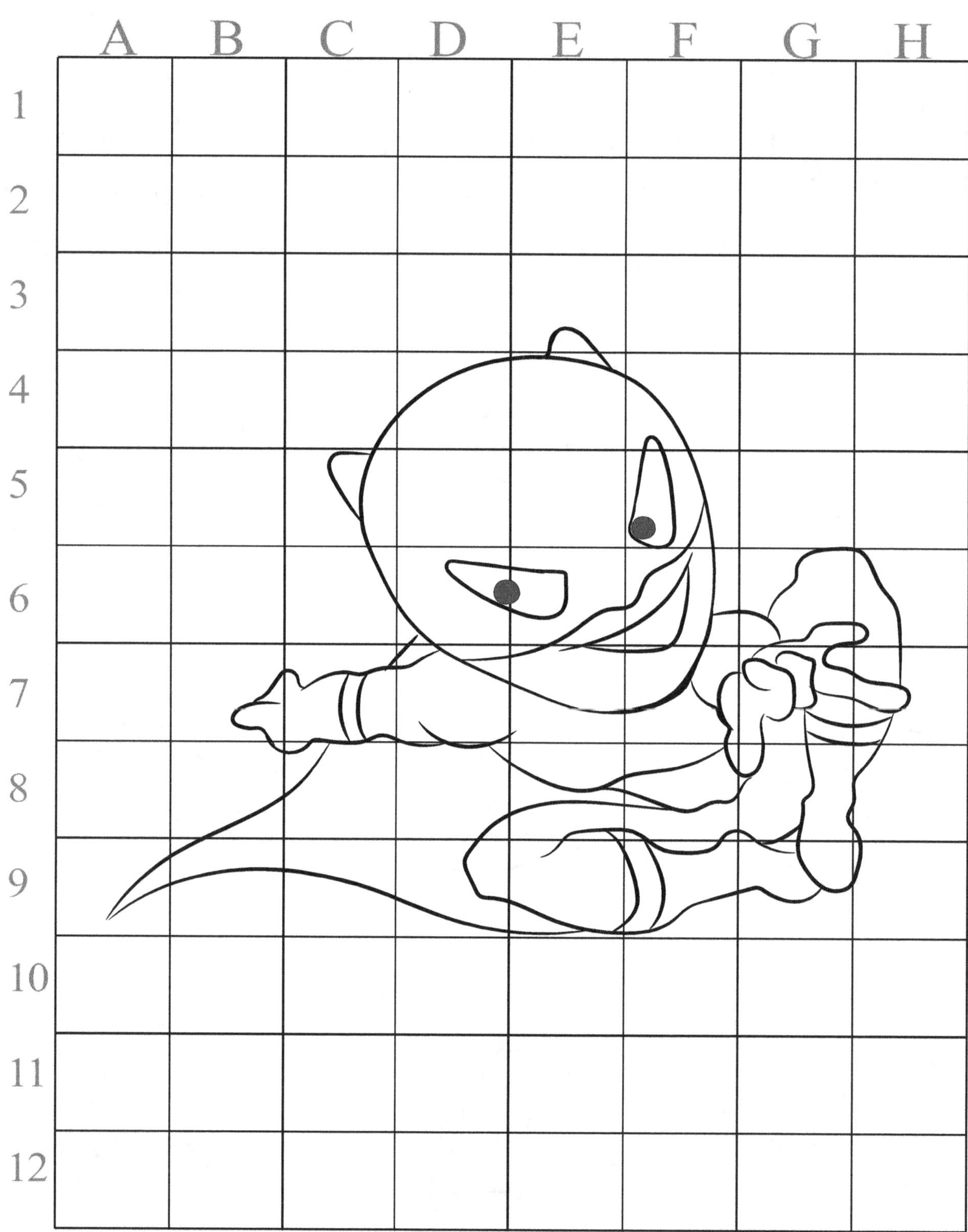
A B C D E F G H
1
2
3
4
5
6
7
8
9
10
11
12

28. Begin by deciding where you want the character's head and major joints to be positioned. Follow this up with the character's limbs.

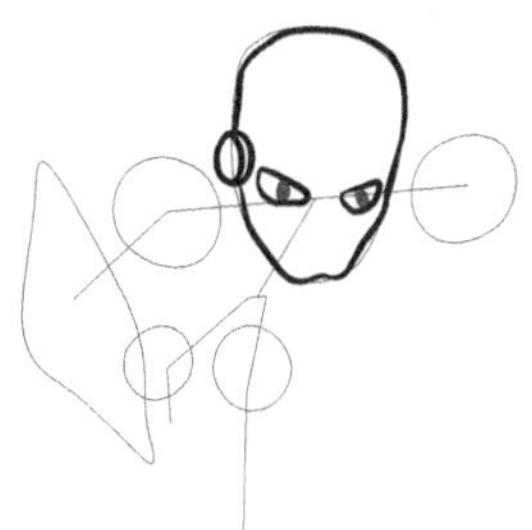

A B C D E F G H
1
2
3
4
5
6
7
8
9
10
11
12

29. Here is another character drawn
from a looked down upon position.

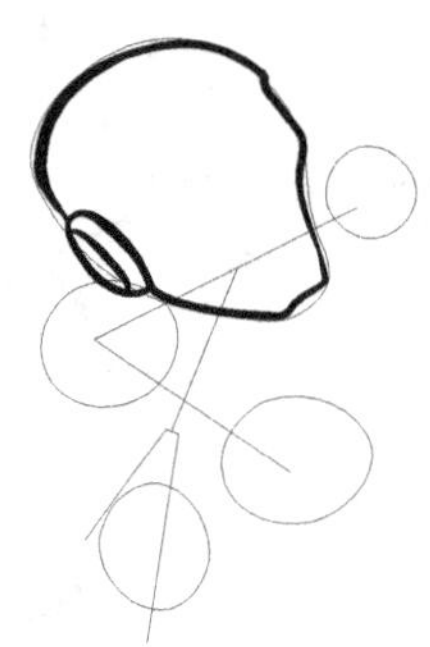

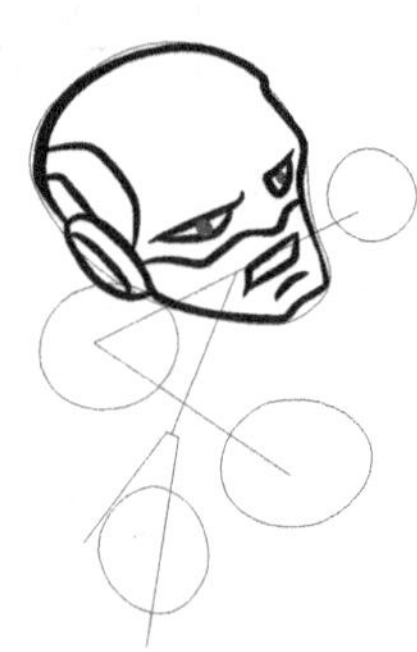

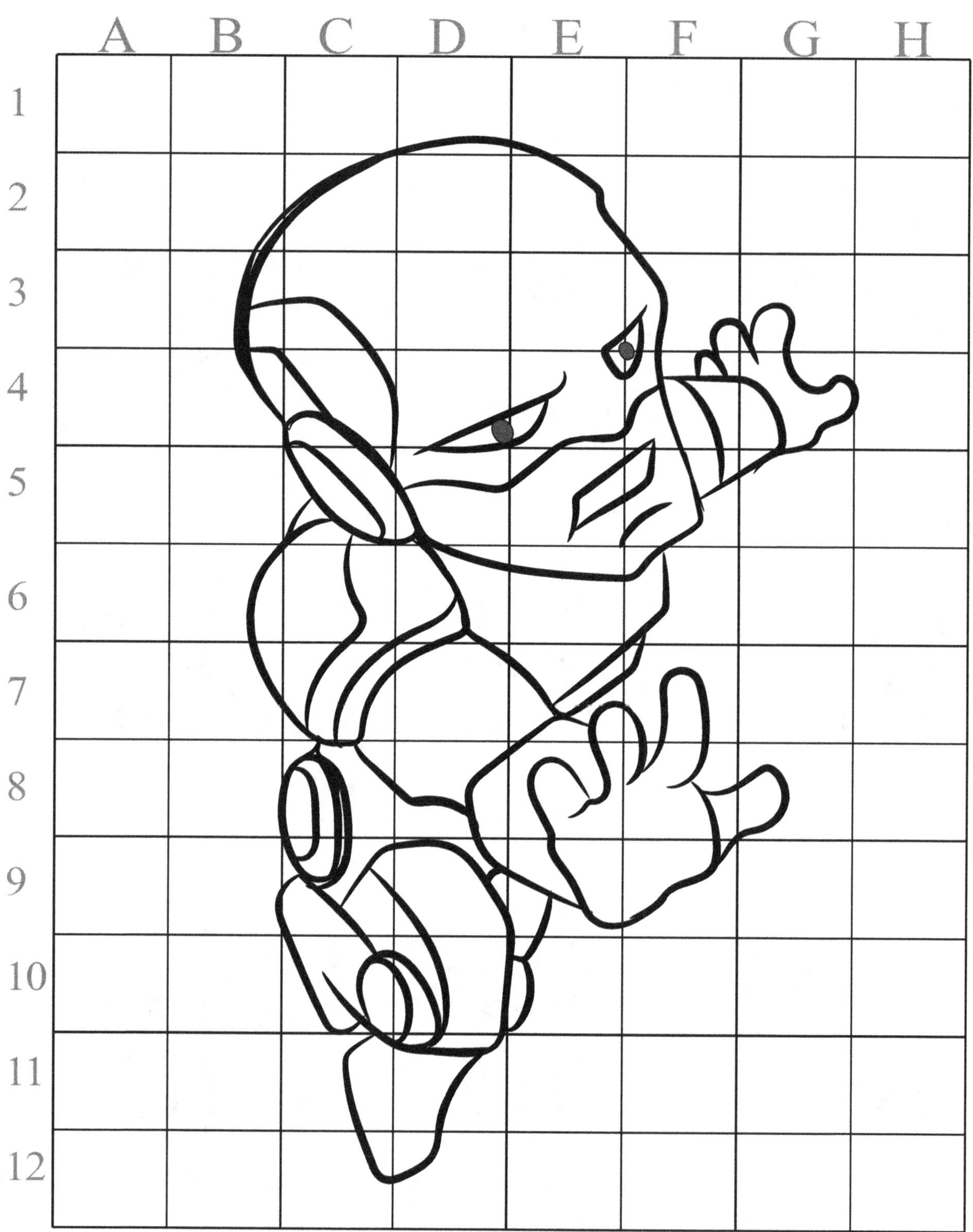

30.   If a project looks too difficult to complete all in one go, complete part of it and come back to it a little later. It will then feel less overwhelming.

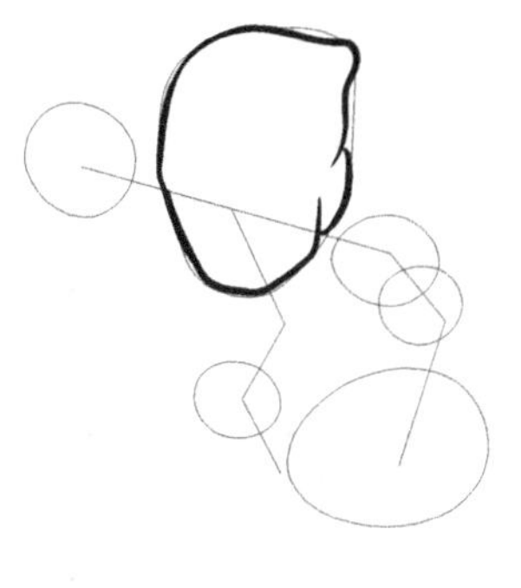

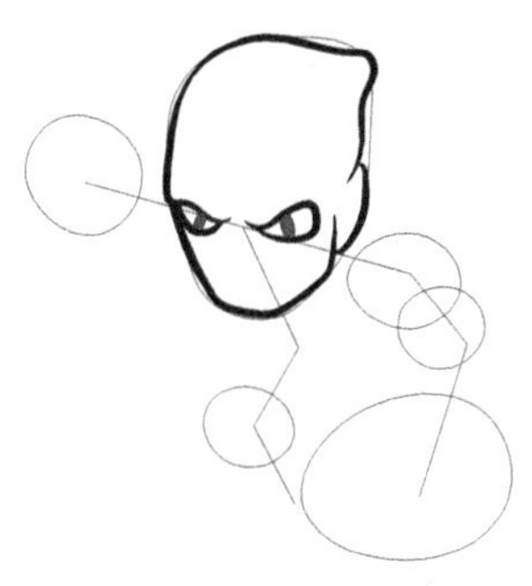

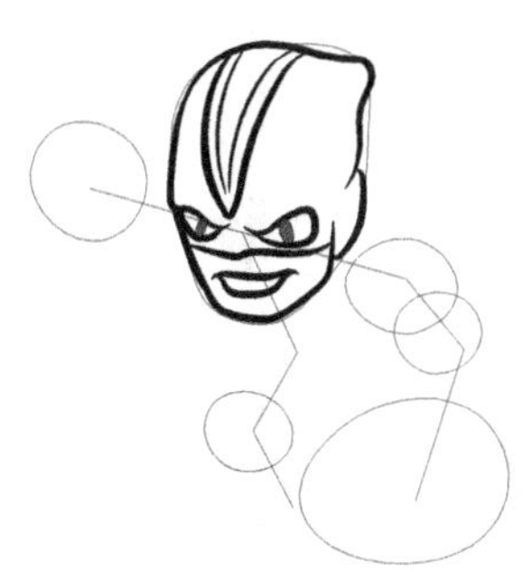

A B C D E F G H
1
2
3
4
5
6
7
8
9
10
11
12

31. Changing your character's proportions can produce some interesting effects.

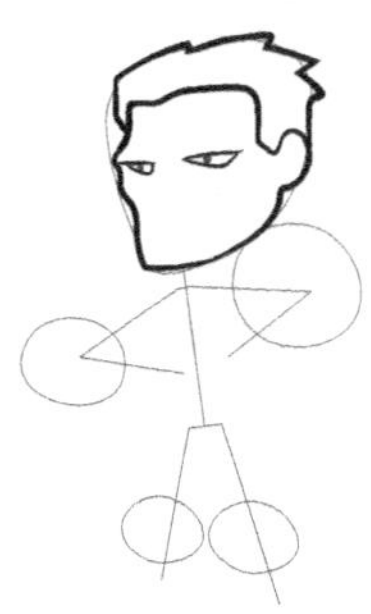

A B C D E F G H
1
2
3
4
5
6
7
8
9
10
11
12

32. If you are struggling for ideas for your work, take a break and do something different. Your mind will keep working in the background for you. Some of our greatest ideas come to us while we sleep

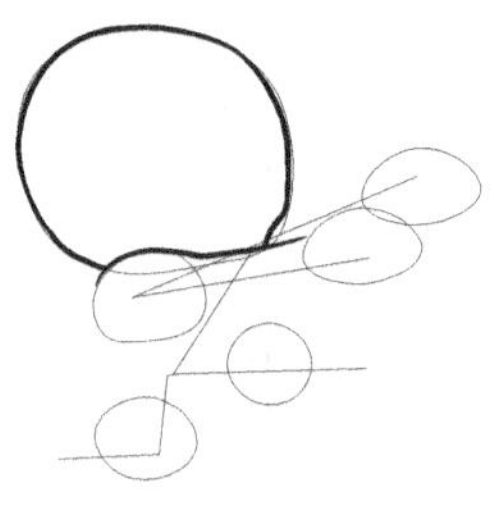 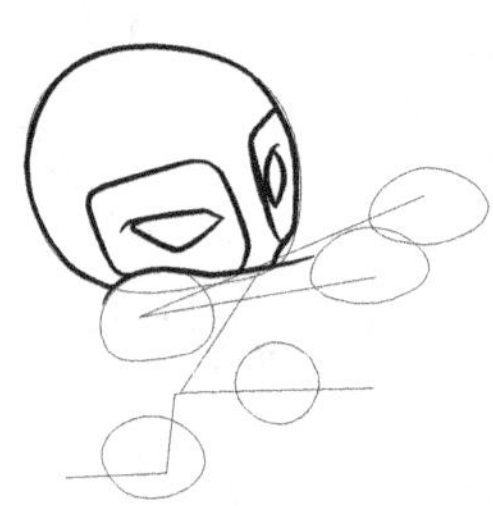 

A B C D E F G H

33. Bending the knees shows even weight distribution and lowers the centre of gravity. This creates greater stability.

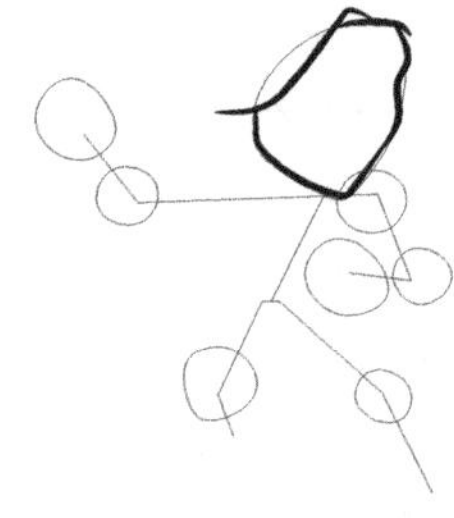

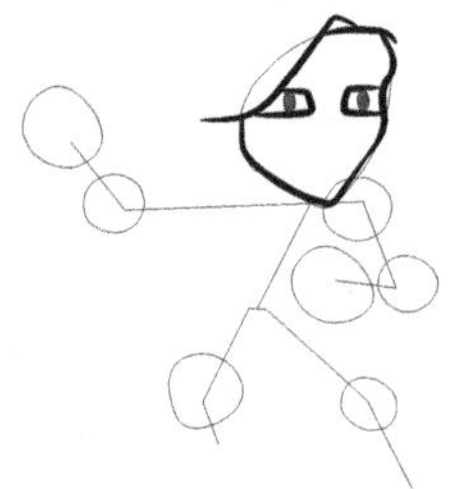

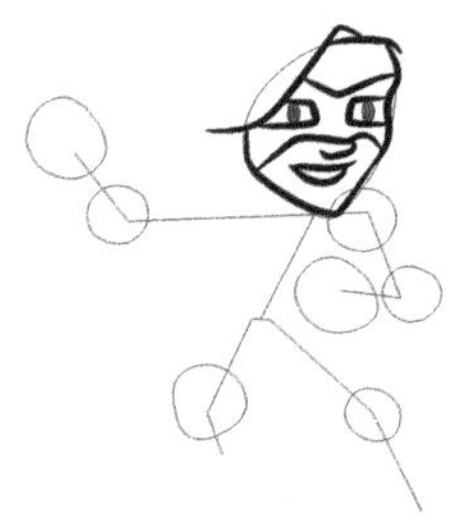

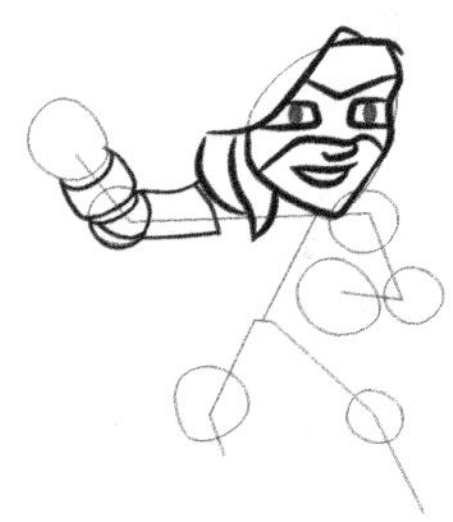

34. A vizor can be very good at concealing your character's true emotions.

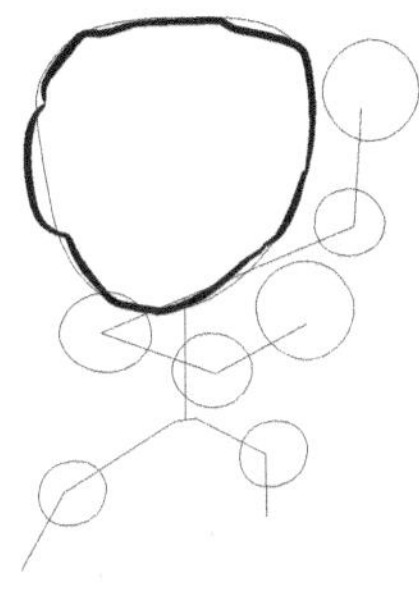 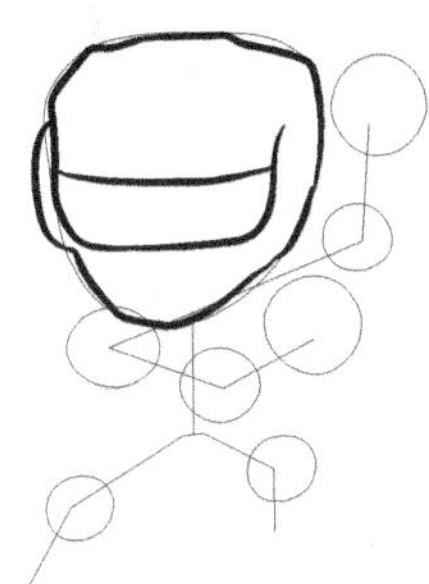 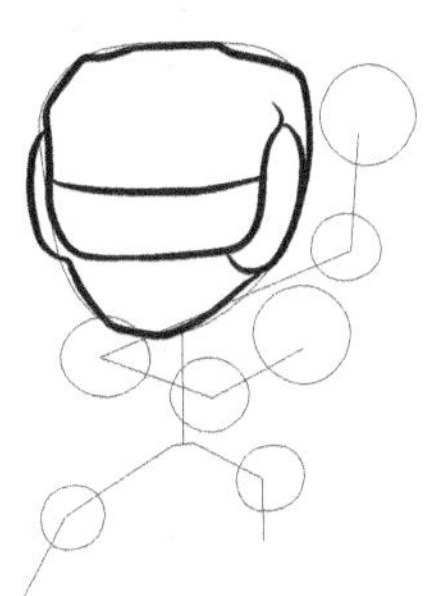

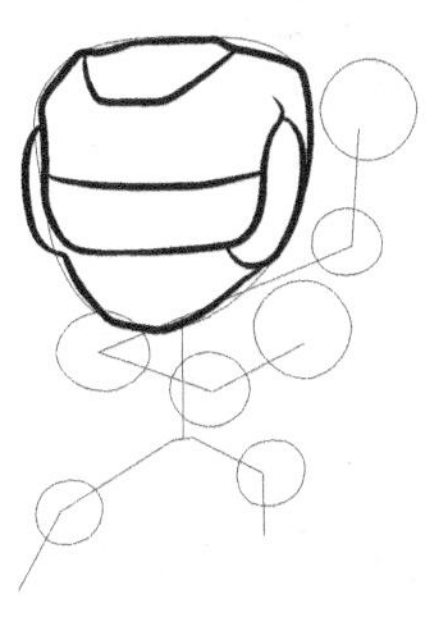 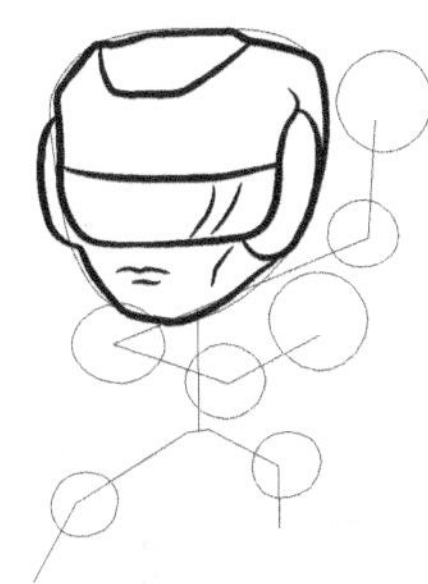 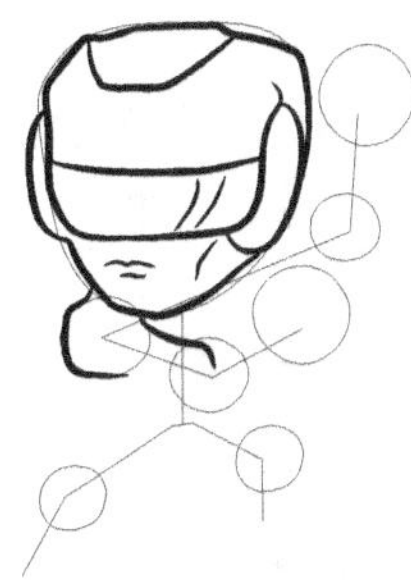

  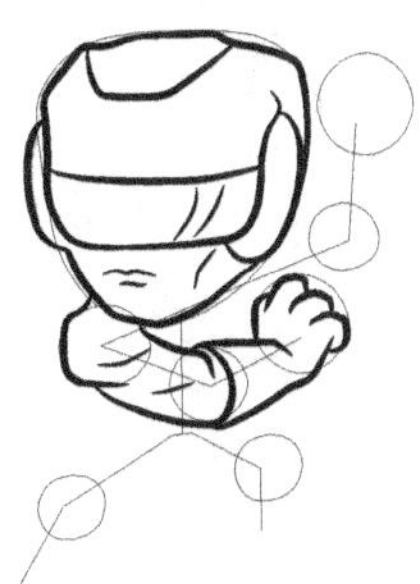

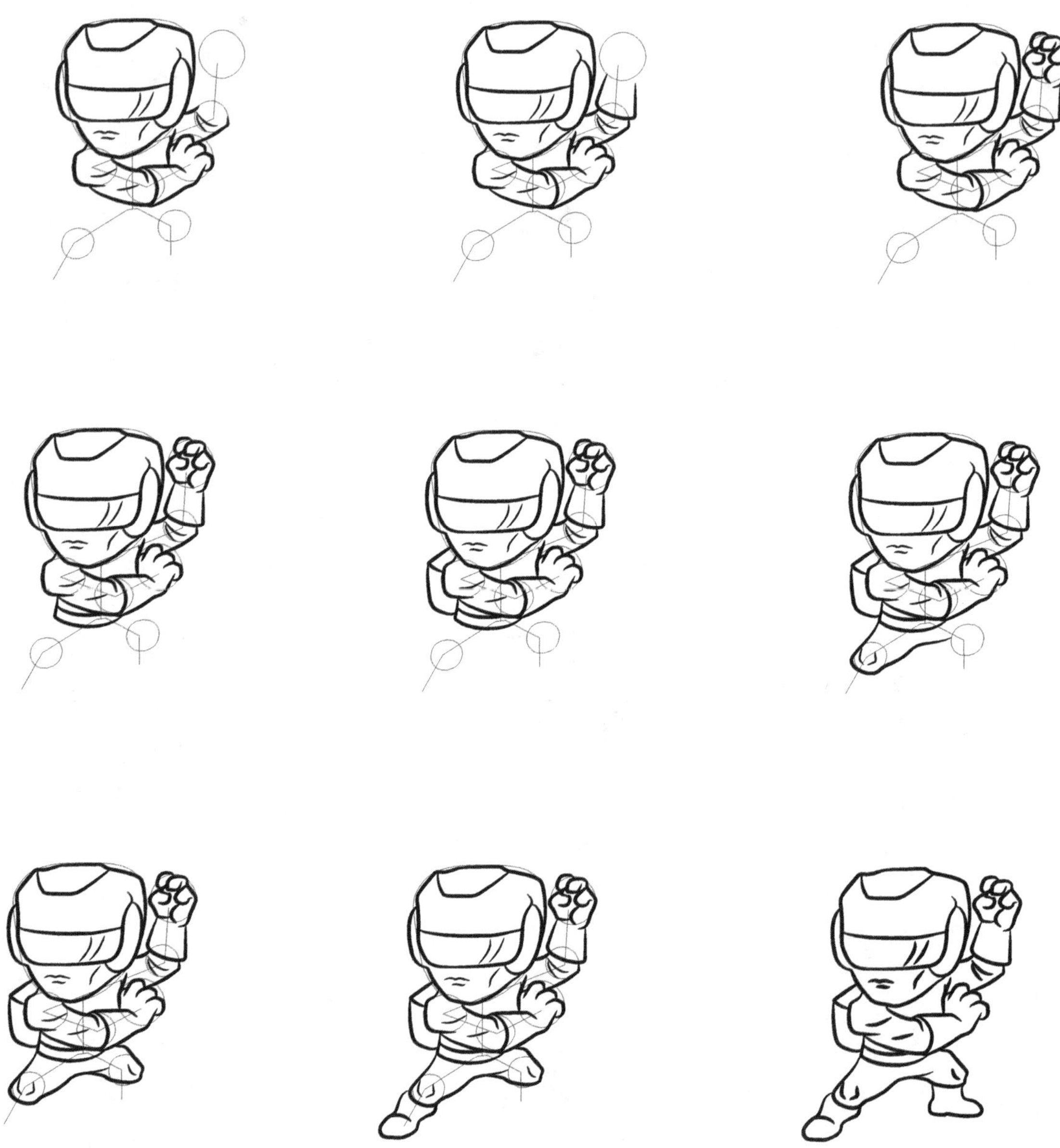

A B C D E F G H

35. If you find that you are rushing, stop what you are doing and take a break. Rushing too much will reduce the quality of your work.

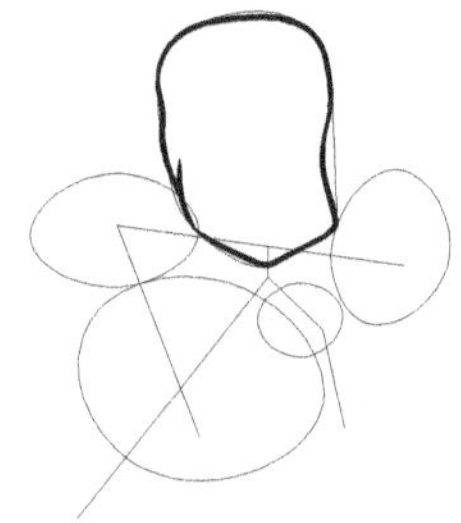 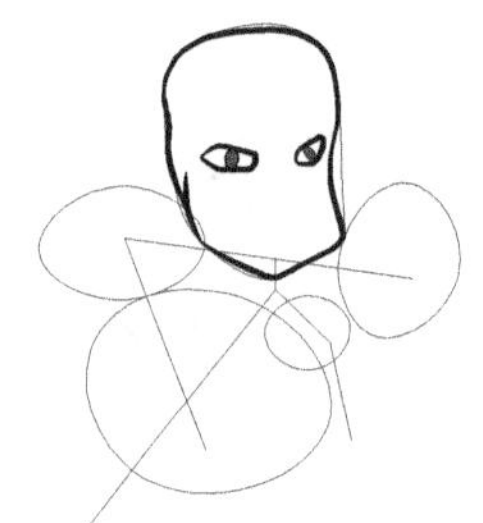 

 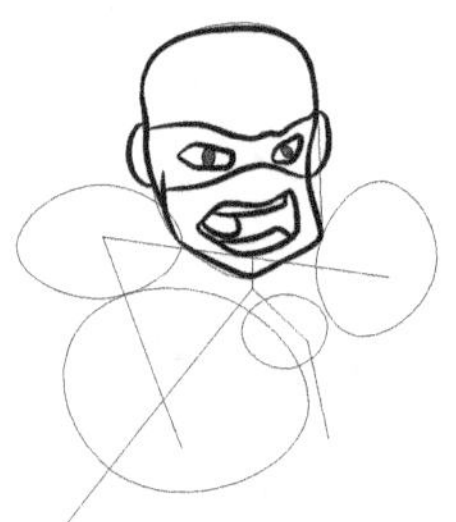 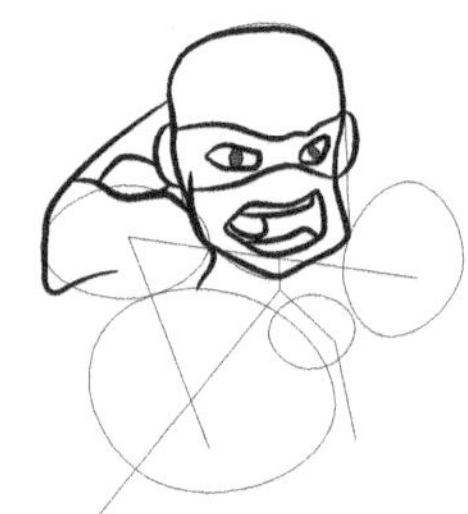

A B C D E F G H
1
2
3
4
5
6
7
8
9
10
11
12

36. Creating a grid with ellipses for the major joints and lines for the major bones can offer a structure to work around.

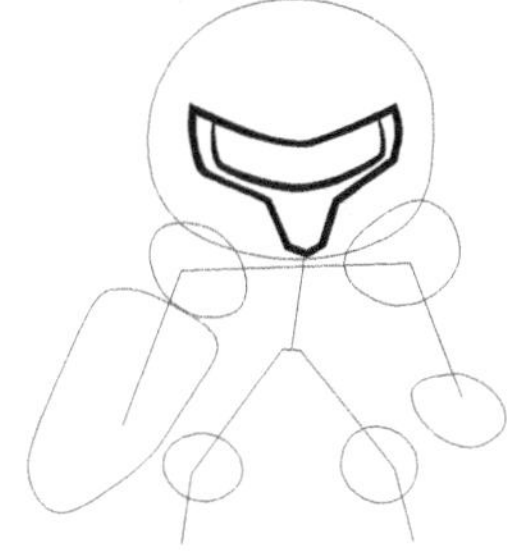

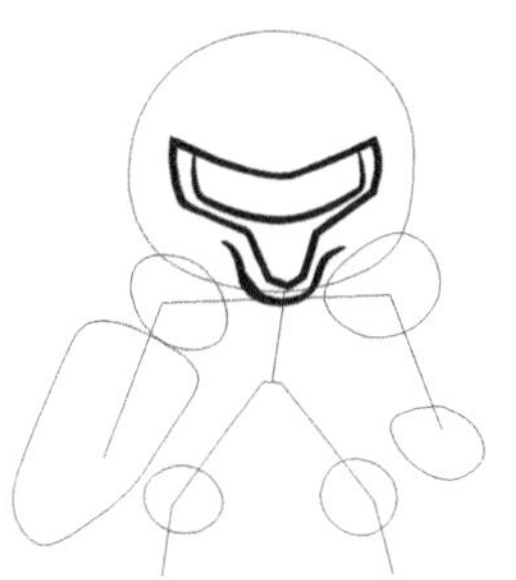

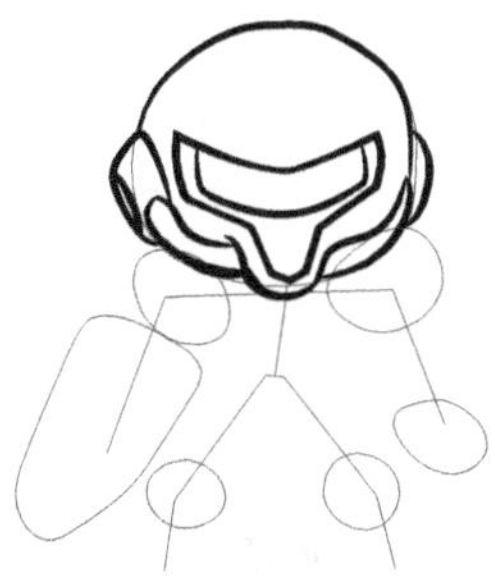

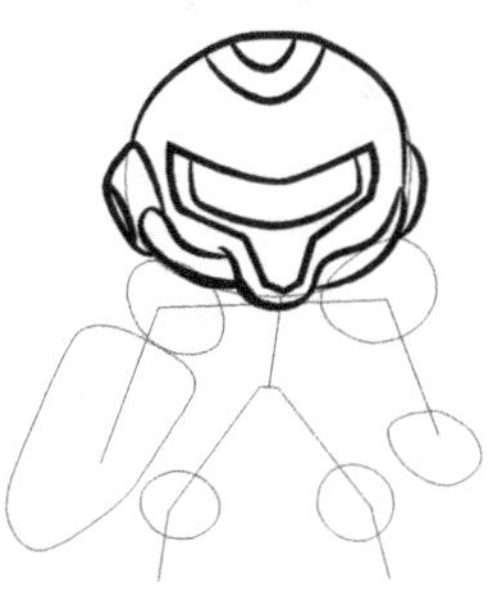

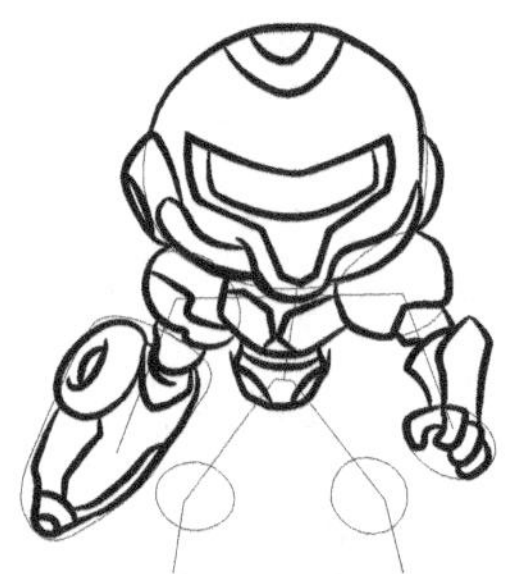

A B C D E F G H
1
2
3
4
5
6
7
8
9
10
11
12

37. How you decide to dress a
character can have a large impact
on how it is interpreted.

 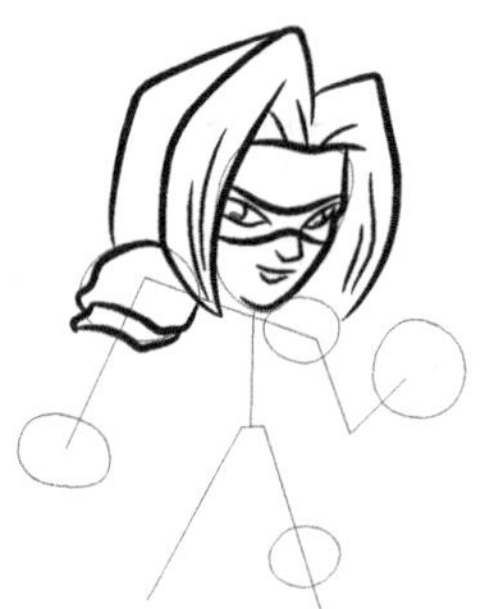 

A B C D E F G H
1
2
3
4
5
6
7
8
9
10
11
12

38. You can create the look of body armour with the addition of just a few lines.

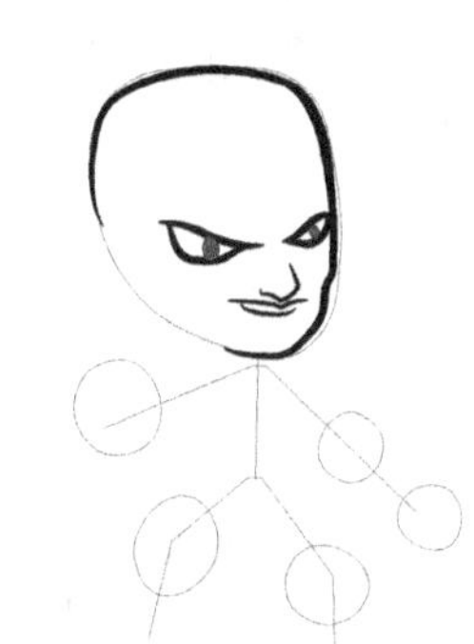

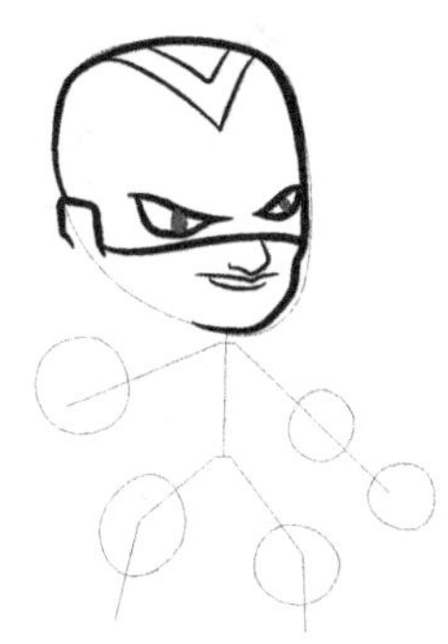

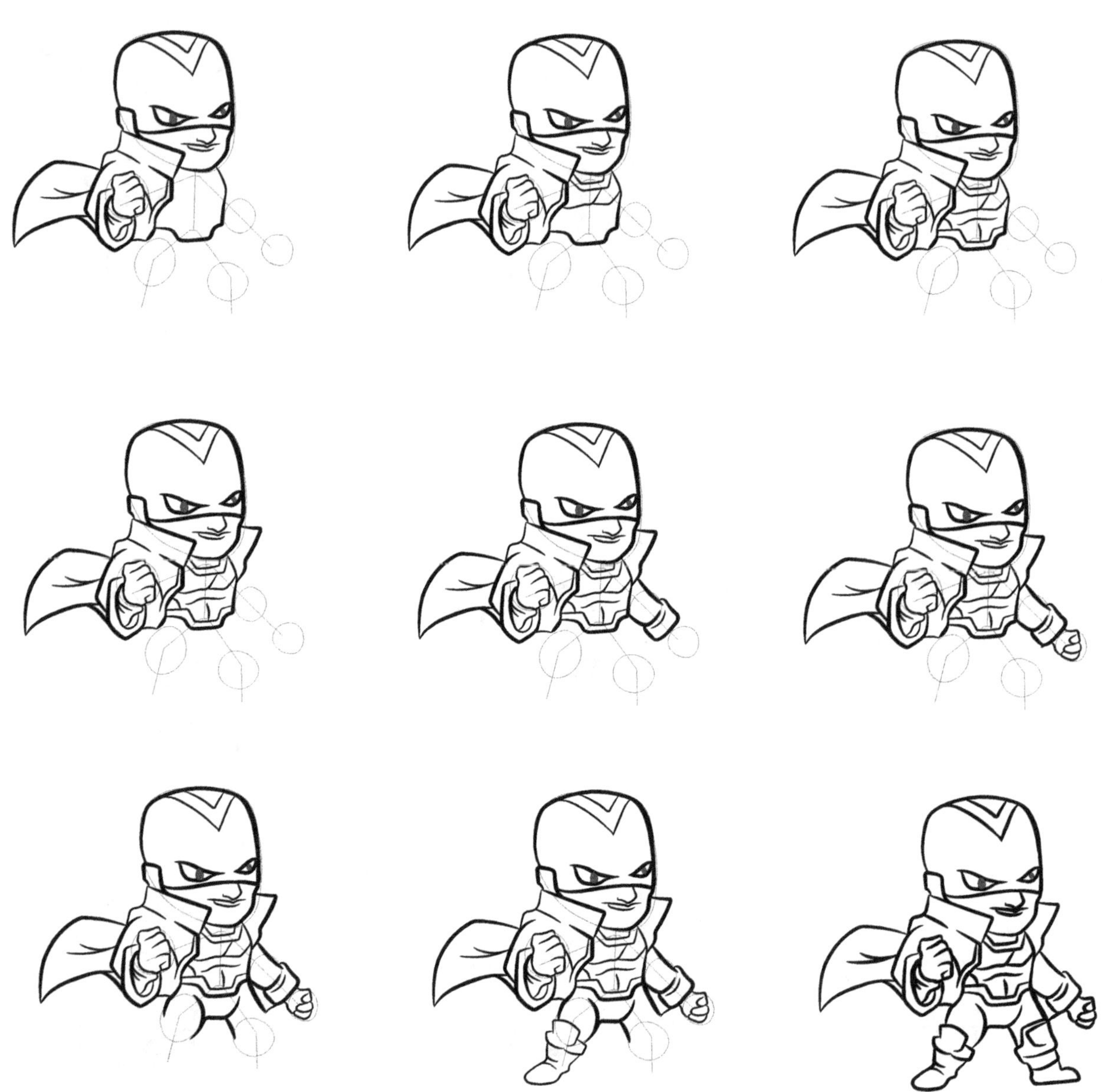

A B C D E F G H
1
2
3
4
5
6
7
8
9
10
11
12

39. A picture paints a
thousand words.

A B C D E F G H
1
2
3
4
5
6
7
8
9
10
11
12

40. Here is an example of
a perspective drawing.

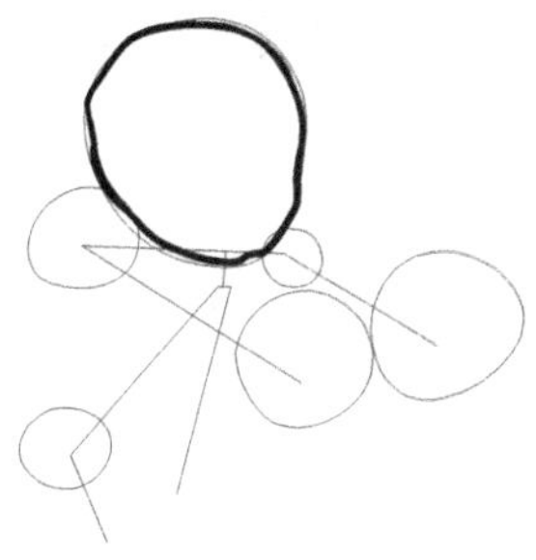
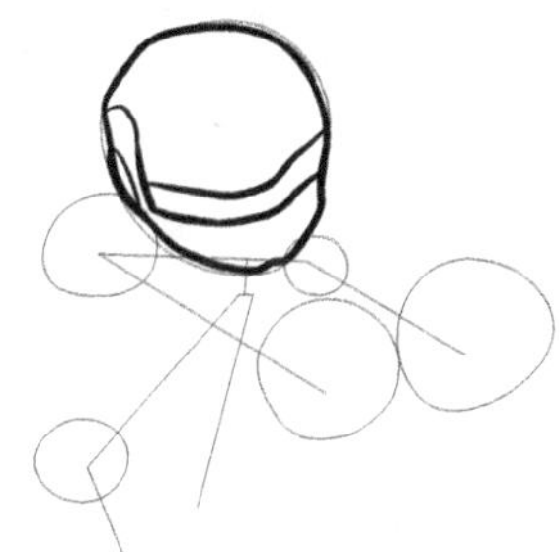
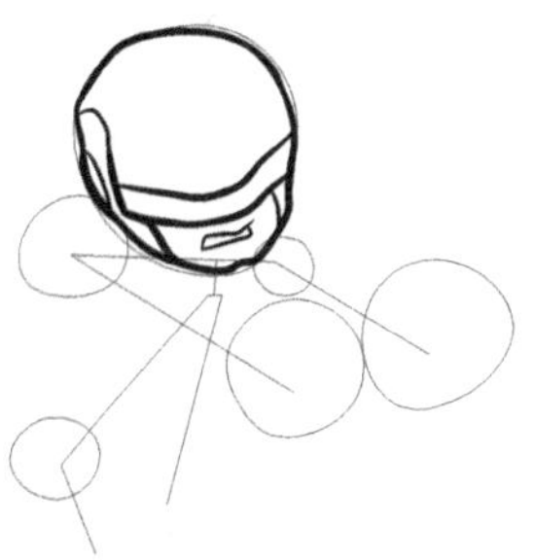

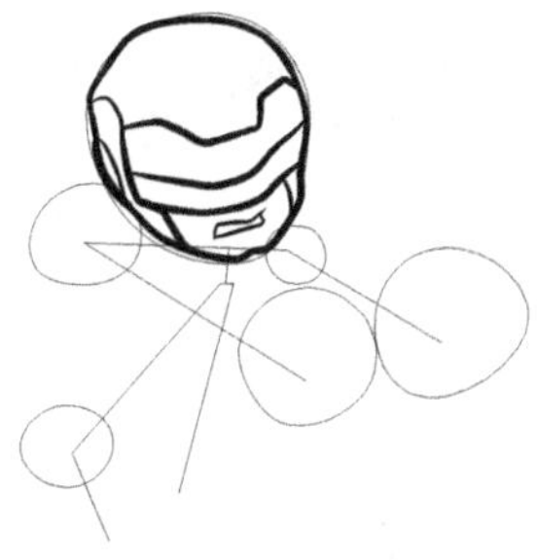
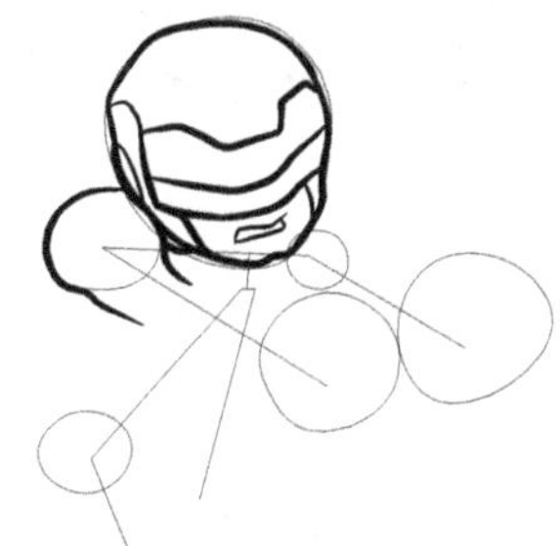
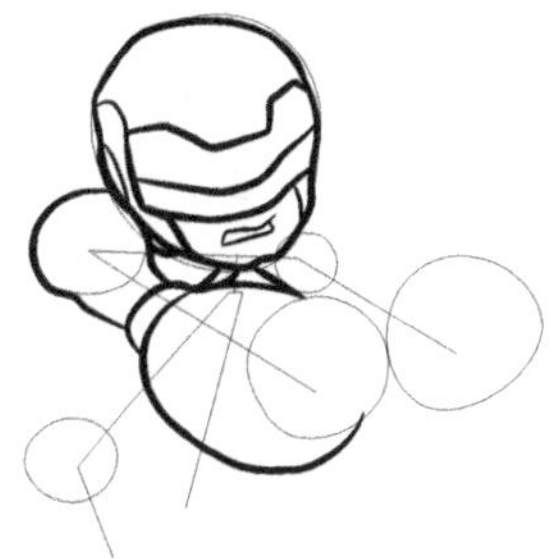